Nothingism

POETS ON POETRY

Derek Pollard, Series Editor
Donald Hall, Founding Editor

TITLES IN THE SERIES

ALSO AVAILABLE, BOOKS BY

Elizabeth Alexander, Meena Alexander, Kazim Ali, A. R. Ammons, John Ashbery, David Baker, Robert Bly, Bruce Bond, Philip Booth, Marianne Boruch, Hayden Carruth, Amy Clampitt, Alfred Corn, Douglas Crase, Robert Creeley, Donald Davie, Thomas M. Disch, Ed Dorn, Martín Espada, Annie Finch, Tess Gallagher, Sandra M. Gilbert, Dana Gioia, Linda Gregerson, Allen Grossman, Thom Gunn, Marilyn Hacker, Rachel Hadas, John Haines, Donald Hall, Joy Harjo, Robert Hayden, Edward Hirsch, Daniel Hoffman, Jonathan Holden, John Hollander, Paul Hoover, Andrew Hudgins, T. R. Hummer, Laura (Riding) Jackson, Josephine Jacobsen, Mark Jarman, Lawrence Joseph, Galway Kinnell, Kenneth Koch, John Koethe, Yusef Komunyakaa, Marilyn Krysl, Maxine Kumin, Martin Lammon (editor), Philip Larkin, David Lehman, Philip Levine, Larry Levis, John Logan, William Logan, David Mason, William Matthews, Joyelle McSweeney, William Meredith, Jane Miller, David Mura, Carol Muske, Alice Notley, Geoffrey O'Brien, Gregory Orr, Alicia Suskin Ostriker, Ron Padgett, Marge Piercy, Grace Schulman, Anne Sexton, Karl Shapiro, Reginald Shepherd, Aaron Shurin, Charles Simic, William Stafford, Anne Stevenson, Cole Swenson, May Swenson, James Tate, Richard Tillinghast, C. K. Williams, Alan Williamson, David Wojahn, Charles Wright, James Wright, John Yau, and Stephen Yenser

For a complete list of titles, please see www.press.umich.edu

Nothingism

Poetry at the End of Print Culture

JASON SCHNEIDERMAN

University of Michigan Press
Ann Arbor

For questions or permissions, please contact um.press.perms@umich.edu

Published in the United States of America by the
University of Michigan Press
Manufactured in the United States of America
Printed on acid-free paper
First published March 2025

A CIP catalog record for this book is available from the British Library.

Library of Congress Cataloging-in-Publication data has been applied for.

ISBN 978-0-472-03984-5 (paper : alk. paper)
ISBN 978-0-472-22210-0 (e-book)

to Elizabeth Scanlon, ideal reader

Contents

Contents

Introduction

This collection of essays represents fifteen years of my best thinking about poetry. For the most part, I have left the essays unchanged, with notable exceptions. All began as essays in *American Poetry Review* under the editorial guidance of Elizabeth Scanlon.

Chapter 1 is a bit of an indulgence. "Nothingism" is a manifesto and asks to be read with a grain of salt; I allowed myself to overstate some claims out of fear that otherwise they might not get stated at all. The manifesto form allowed me to be a bit bolder in my claims about attention and poetry than I might otherwise have been.

Having gotten that diatribe out of my system, I return to a more measured and scholarly pose for chapter 2, which traces the history of the poetic line in English and puts forth my own theory of the line. As a scholar-poet, I consider my theorization of the line to be my most important contribution to field of poetics. Because it gathers so much under one chapter heading, the section titles may allow the time strapped reader to find their point of interest without getting too overwhelmed.

The sonnet has been a longstanding obsession, thanks to my having been a student of Phillis Levin, and chapter 3 allows me to make an argument about how the sonnet has shifted in the last two generations of American writers. In suggesting a change in the sonnet's structure, I am suggesting a change in how we understand ourselves.

Chapter 4 is a consideration of inaugural poems that I wrote during the first Obama administration. I chose not to update the essay. The condition of poetry and politics have changed so much that I felt that my only choices were to leave the essay as written or start from scratch. This has actually been a rather popular essay, so I present it here as it was written. I suspect it will be of sociological interest to younger readers curious about the poetry and politics of the not-so-distant past. I have added a postscript considering how much things have changed.

Chapter 5, an essay on teaching, confronted me with the same choice as chapter 4. In this case, I wrote something completely new. I have retained the title, "A Rising Tide Floats All Boats," because I still believe that a good classroom advances all learners. The original version of this essay reflected my questions and struggles in the classroom. A decade of teaching later, I have answers and solutions. The chapter presents ten principles I've learned from being in front of various classrooms (in person and online). I hope that chapter 5 can stand alone, and that it will be helpful to anyone who is called upon to teach, or who takes up teaching as a calling.

Chapters 6 and 7 are quite personal. Chapter 7 is about the mentoring friendship of James Merrill and Agha Shahid Ali. Chapter 7 is an act of love, designed to keep Ali's work in the world, and follows the example of Ali himself, who taught Merrill's work in order to keep Merrill in the world. Chapter 6 explores Merrill's long poem, *The Changing Light at Sandover*, and my fascination with how it presents the act of writing itself.

I chose the subtitle "Poetry at the End of Print Culture" because these essays have all been inflected by a move away from poetry as a printed object toward poetry as a digital object. When I began publishing, online publications did not "count." At the beginning of my life as a poet, the internet was a way to communicate about what really mattered: printed publications. Even online submissions were a novelty. I've been using Submittable since it was called Submishmash. But poetry is not isolated from the world or the culture in which it is written and read. In 2001, a series of anthrax-by-mail attacks accelerated online submissions as a norm. The dangers of the physical were enacted again during lockdown as Zoom allowed us to avoid transmitting COVID. New media has a way of starting as a more convenient version of an older media, before it reshapes that older media, and then recasts the older media as its precursor. If mid-century office memos *look* like proto-emails, then it remains to be seen what today's emails will look like to the future. In seeing what has already changed, we might see both the present and past more clearly. Ideally, we will be more ready for the future. Fortunately, the position of poetry looks strong.

I fear that thanking anyone will mean that I am leaving out someone, but I must thank the people who have brought me to this point. I have been incredibly fortunate to live my life alongside Ada Limón, Jennifer

L. Knox, Erika Meitner, Kathleen Volk Miller, and Marion Wrenn. Friendship is a conversation. Be careful: If you start talking to me, we might never stop. The mentorship of Tom Sleigh, Phillis Levin, and Thomas Mallon have shaped me in ways for which I am daily grateful. The brilliant copy editing of Jonathan Schneiderman has improved this book significantly. (He would have advised me to remove the adjective "brilliant" had he been given the chance, and he probably would have been right, but I'm leaving it in anyway.) Rachel Zucker, Kazim Ali, Jericho Brown, and Gregory Pardlo have been intrepid fellow travelers. John Deming and Jada Gordon have been dear friends and collaborators. Kate Gale, Tobi Harper, and Mark Cull have given my poetry a home at Red Hen Press, without which I would feel adrift (as I did before I met them). Much of this volume was completed while on a Fulbright to the University of Nottingham, and I am grateful for the support of the Fulbright Foundation, the University of Nottingham, and the warm embrace of my new British friends and colleagues (especially the Nottingham Front Runners). The Borough of Manhattan Community College has been my professional home for nearly fifteen years. As much as I complain about being overworked, I am grateful to have that work. My students have kept me on my toes and made me see with new eyes each semester. I could not ask for better colleagues than Geoff Klock, Syreeta McFadden, Holly Messitt, Lol Fow, Rifat Salam, and Claire Pamplin. I am also grateful to teach in the MFA Program for Writers at Warren Wilson College, where some of these essays began as lectures and classes.

I am deeply grateful to Derek Pollard for his interest in this book, to Haley Winkle for guiding it through the publication process, and to the University of Michigan Press for believing in my work enough to make it into an exemplar of my favorite medium of all time: a book.

And finally, whether you are holding a codex or reading on a screen, I am grateful for you, reader. Your time and attention are not taken for granted by this author.

Nothingism

A Manifesto

Writing seems to be approaching the condition of speech, and perhaps it's merely nostalgia for print culture, but it feels nefarious to me. If Marshall McLuhan was right, and the "medium is the message," then the speed at which online communication seems to be circulating outrage and jealousy (with an intensity that is hardly unprecedented) will only increase, and the intensity of fury one had hoped would pass as the medium "matured," whatever that means, will persist. (Clearly digital or "post-print" culture is not terribly mature, and this lack of maturity seems to rub off onto those who engage it.) Even though the internet came to us through the military and the academy, the internet has kept its initial values of speed and immediacy without the accompanying values of its creating institutions: hierarchy, decorum, rigor, apprenticeship, analysis, evidence, respect. We have allowed a century of regulation to collapse as we welcome "disruption"; we have devalued expertise in favor of crowdsourcing; we have devalued the physical in favor of pixels; we have devalued revision and precision in favor of immediate response. Headlines are not the stuff of morning and evening, but round-the-clock intrusions. Any engagement with the tiny computer we still call a "phone" brings an us-versus-them array of crises and disasters (real, dire, misleading, fake, and manufactured). Unsuccessfully, I keep trying to turn these "updates" off.

Reflection is not action. I trust reflection, and I do not trust action. When I was a child, my father would tell me a military saying that escapes me now. The essence of the adage was that, often, an answer is needed before you have time to formulate one. Naturally, I became a poet in response, the sort of person who can delay answering a question for as long as needed. Sometimes the delay is only as long as a sonnet. Sometimes the delay is as long as a career. Sometimes the answer is never produced, and why should it be? Aren't some questions worth pondering for a lifetime, in the euphoric manner of Socrates, rather than hammered to the wall in the plodding manner of Aristotle? I have little patience for fake questions, the kitsch of overcoming, sentimental celebrations of human triumph, chipper self-determination in the guise of nature worship, or cheap faith. Any true faith is agonizing, beset by doubt, guilt, and fear. Any true faith brings only slivers of comfort, small slices of peace before the pain demands contemplation yet again. What was that again about afflicting the comfortable? Action cannot be avoided. One publishes a book, eats a meal, takes a job, attends a meeting, lifts some weights, takes a shower. One wakes up to change the baby's diaper or to soothe a pensive lover. But still, action is valorized beyond its due. A friend of mine introduced to me the phrase, "Don't just do something, stand there." She is a very good friend.

Life, in the age of digital communication, has come to feel unrehearsed to me. Or to be more precise: life has come to feel like a play that is under-rehearsed. In the days when I wanted to be an actor, because I wanted more than anything to escape the confines of my life, I was in plays in which no one knew their lines. I was once in a production of *Cat on a Hot Tin Roof* that went so wrong, none of us were ever quite sure when it was over. The scenes bled into each other, and we were cast in ways that seem almost comically cruel. The one actor required to sing a few lines of a song was tone deaf in a way that made even a few bars of "By the Light of the Silvery Moon" unrecognizable. You could tell he was trying to sing, and yet what happened on stage was not something anyone could call singing. If anyone paused too long, the actress playing Big Momma would just scream, "Nobody's gonna give Big Daddy morphine" and we'd proceed from there, sometimes multiple times in a single performance. The extended dialogue of act II, almost entirely unknown to the two performers, once went on so long that the rest of us just walked in and began performing act III. This is what "citizen journalism" feels like to me. This is what politics on Twitter feel like to me. This is what poetry on Facebook feels like to me. It's not that you can't see what it's supposed to be; it's that your time is being wasted, but you're stuck sitting through it out of some loyalty to the incompetents stumbling about on stage, bad accents and all. Every time someone calls a literary editor a "gatekeeper" rather than a "curator," a little part of me dies. Yes, why bother going to the Guggenheim or the MoMA? There are sidewalks and card tables with artists setting up their art. Do people really want only sidewalks and card tables? Do they think that curators never visit sidewalks and card tables?

Poetry, more than any other medium (even, I think, playwriting), aspires to the sounds and rhythms of speech. Or poetry aspires to what speech could be. In the ur-art that existed before genre division, we speculate that speech and music and dance were all heightened and stylized together in ways that were not separate from worship. I have no nostalgia for this ur-art. I'm glad to have my poems set to music, but I don't want any nonsense about how Bob Dylan or Bruce Springsteen (or Sting) lyrics are poems, when they are clearly incomplete without melody. I care about the way that paper and ink have offered a process of composition that begins in gestation, proceeds through drafts, and ends in publication, composed for the spoken voice to be read in silence or out loud. On screens, drafts have no reality. On screens, as in speech, what is gone has disappeared. Everything pixel-based is infinitely revisable, but also infinitely presentable—presuming you managed to screen-shot it before it disappeared. In print culture, there were often many versions, but each had a paper reality, and it was in tension with speech. Now my students see no difference between turning in a paper and linking me to a Google Doc. Now my students are silent at the start of class, talking not to each other, but texting people they already know. There is no need to learn new ways of speaking as they disappear deeper into the silence of the screens that anticipate their words and type for them so that they barely even have to move their fingers.

I've noticed that my positive feelings are in direct proportion to the length of my reading material. After a book, I feel surprisingly good—thoroughly engaged and well informed. Long-form journalism and articles give me a similar sense of wellbeing, or at least of a thorough understanding. However, on the days when I read just headlines, I feel dizzy and furious. Sometimes I glimpse a push notification of a headline that links to an article I cannot open, and I devolve into panic trying to find the substance behind the willfully misleading provocation. And yet I read fewer books and more headlines—which is like saying I eat more potato chips than baked potatoes, or I eat more M&Ms than bars of chocolate—how could I not? I spend less time in contemplation and more time chasing items off my ever-expanding to-do list, while being driven to distraction by clickbait headlines. But here is the rub. I continue to click in anger, so disgusted by the article's very existence that I feel compelled to see it for myself. Somewhere, my desire for evidence was turned against me.

In response, I have decided to invent a new movement: Nothingism. If you feel overwhelmed, emotionally and physically, you may too be a budding Nothingist. Nothingists indulge their nostalgia for print culture, and Nothingists value print as a lasting object. Nothingism celebrates the isolation of reading, and turns off its wi-fi, and leaves its phone at home. Nothingism insists on a divide between print and speech that is blurred and mutual, but also real and powerful. Although I am the first Nothingist to call myself a Nothingist, I am a bad Nothingist. I present Nothingism as an ideal, and like so many before me, I fear that I am unable to live up to the ideals I espouse precisely because I am espousing them. After all, who bothers to espouse ideals they don't need to be reminded to live up to?

I have always wanted an audience—but I have also wanted the audience to be at the same remove from me as I am from the writers I love. I never expected to be retweeted by Kafka or to have Gwendolyn Brooks respond to my e-mail so that I could impress my high school teacher by including an amusing anecdote about what happened on the night she finished "We Real Cool." In reading, I feel an intense intimacy with the author, but I never mistake that intimacy for friendship or acquaintance. When I gave readings for my first book, people would often ask me if my husband was all right, and my first reaction was to panic and say, "What happened?" Nothing had happened. They were reacting to my book about having an HIV positive partner, a book I'd written years before its publication. They felt close to me, but it was uni-directional. I felt like my book had succeeded, but that I had failed. I have considered going the full Elena Ferrante, who may be the most committed Nothingist of all time. But it's too late for me to truly disappear into my work, to slide off of all digital media, remaining only in the printed pages I savor. And I like giving readings and going to readings—to hear the poems out loud is a pleasure I would never want to surrender. A Nothingist refuses to surrender a pleasure.

I have always wanted less of the world, or rather, for there to be less.

Elizabeth Bishop, with her nearly perfect lifetime output collected into a slender volume, seemed so much preferable to those massive doorstops that are most celebrated poets' final repository of poems. Has anyone ever truly loved one of those doorstops, so massive that your legs would lose circulation just from resting it in your lap? Of course this preference for less is an indefensible position. If I find James Merrill's work prior to *Sandover* a bit too calculated, or if I find late Ted Hughes a bit ponderous, so what? No one is holding a gun to my head; I don't have to read anything I don't want to. And yet. To keep up. To be current. To have a historical perspective. To be an expert. To wittily comment on Twitter or Facebook or Instagram in that knowing way that wafts a lifetime of erudition and microblogging acumen. Isn't that how one gets a book contract these days? Is there another way to find readers?

And what of productivity? We are so addicted to work, to output, to improvement. How did "revolutionary" stop describing the effort to overthrow an existing government to create a differently envisioned government and start describing what we want from our next iPhone, or our next gadget? Even Foucault brags about his work ethic, while bemoaning the internal demands to be a good bourgeois subject. What part of our lizard brain demands cheap energy, expensive clothing, and box stores in which we can buy enough detergent to last six months in a single oversized bottle? Am I the only one driven to exhaustion by the push push push of productivity? Why did I not obey Grace Paley's commandment to keep a low overhead? Why is college celebrated as an opportunity to increase one's earning power, rather than an opportunity for reflection and the slowness of problem solving? Hooray, we've made so many cars, our planet is headed toward being uninhabitable! Hooray, I worked a twelve-hour day so I can sleep in expensive sheets on an expensive bed! Isn't productivity part of what is killing us? Would cheaper sheets be so bad?

Is it so wrong to want poetry to be counterproductive? To quite literally—as Auden wrote—make nothing happen? I've scoffed at those who see poetry as somehow revolutionary in the Marxist sense, at those who see poetry as a way out of capitalism or class or privilege or entitlement. (There is not a way out of these things, only a reckoning with them.) I see the academy as the greatest patron that poetry has ever had, and yet it requires me to teach an awful lot of composition classes. How did my love of poetry lead me to spending my days telling students about topic sentences and the differences between citation styles? Today we are told over and over that all poetry is political. But these voices don't mean the word "political" the way that Nothingism does. Before the popularized slogan was "The personal is political," the second-wave feminist slogan was iterated as "The political is personal." This distinction is everything to a Nothingist. Funding for health care, voting rights, gun control, rent control, free college tuition—these are all political concerns that are immensely personal. But this is not the same as saying that everything is political. Isn't the point of free tuition that everyone can make a personal choice as to whether or not college is right for them? Isn't the point of fighting for reproductive rights that you can make personal choices without juridical intrusion? Is not the search for an ideal politics a search for the politics that would free us to enjoy the personal? For the Nothingist, politics must have an outside in order for there to be such a thing as politics—the Nothingist says that if everything is politics, then nothing is politics. When I read, my body is expending the energy I generated by eating a meal; that does not make reading a form of eating. Nothingism votes, but a vote is not a poem. Nothingism demands that we be a part-time everything.

What Nothingism bemoans, of late—what I am bemoaning—is the end of reflection. The end of a process that culminates in a final product. Nothingism resists the endless "Here's where I am now" that properly belongs to intimate spaces, rather than public ones. Nothingism insists on intimacy as the opposite of "public." When we complain of the constant campaign in our politics, wishing for a government that would govern with the best interest of all its citizens at heart, we are wishing for reflection. When we bemoan the endless hunger for non-fiction that seems to crowd out fiction, we are wishing for imagination. When we bemoan the "poetry" that has been prefixed with "insta," we are bemoaning instancy itself—the brief snippets of language, offering repetitive iterations of shallow self-adoration that begin with the premise of radically empowered independence that in turn leads to a ferocious rejection of the painful realities of interdependence. We must retreat from the social and return to the social, but the retreat must be to a productive space of contemplation. "Scrolling" has become a metaphor for how we read online, the "page" endlessly opening up onto the "bottomless trough"—

but what of the literal scrolls, the rolled-up papyri in Alexandria? The language of writing is endlessly repurposed for the medium that devalues it, the internet desperate not for articles or poems or interviews, but "content." Contemplation is a name I offer for poetry. Privacy is a name I offer for poetry. Nothingism is a name I offer for poetry.

When commercial photography was nascent, Kodak invented "the Kodak moment" to teach consumers how to need a camera in order to remember their own lives—lives which had been remembered without the help of photography since the beginning of human memory. Then, for almost one hundred years, people took photographs, without knowing what they would look like when developed, looked at them later, and saved them in books to review nostalgically. Now with another commercial shift, we take photos for immediate distribution to tell everyone else what we are doing, and then never look at them again. Nothingism fears that poems are being spun off into disposability on a parallel track to photography. Nothingism prefers to remember the event without the intrusion. Nothingism is angry about the hours wasted in the wasteland of images offered up on social media, and prefers to read a book, to meet a friend in person, ideally to discuss the poems that we read on paper. Nothingism is not surprised at how often the most popular poems on the internet are plagiarized.

I offer Nothingism in the spirit that O'Hara offered Personism. As he wrote, when you are being chased, you run, rather than explaining your athletic credentials to your pursuer. But what good are the erotics of Personism in a world where being Lucky Pierre is not the serendipitous result of an unlikely set of encounters following an evening of movie-going, but an explicitly requested act on Grindr, fulfilled within an hour or two, as people respond, "I am only looking for muscle twinks within a fifty-foot radius of my favorite coffee shop because I can't be inconvenienced by surprise, chance, or unexpected possibility." Indeed, the chance offered by O'Hara's city has been reduced to an endless menu of predictable pleasures: People who ordered this book on Amazon also ordered these books. People who liked this film on Netflix also liked these films. Facebook offers you hundreds of people to endorse your bad behavior and reassure you that it wasn't bad behavior at all. But if I want to hear Cyndi Lauper performing "When You Were Mine" I have to get out my old CD because that song (and that song only) has been scrubbed from the Spotify version of *She's So Unusual*.[1] Nothingism, like Frankie, says relax. Nothingism says keep what you love nearby. Nothingism says welcome chance. Nothingism says we need a new erotics of patience, a new erotics of inaction. Nothingism says stay in and read tonight. Maybe I'll come over later and we can cuddle on the couch. Nothingism says wait long enough and you'll be dead. Nothingism says, with Whitman, if you're reading this, then I'm here with you now, and can't that be enough for both of us? For now, I mean. Just until the end of this sentence.

Note

1. This is no longer true. Following Prince's death, his entire catalog showed up on Spotify, including Lauper's cover of "When You Were Mine." However, the point remains—perhaps best illustrated by the disappearance of Orwell's *1984* and *Animal Farm* from all Kindles in 2009. The digital universe makes it appear that everything is available, with the result that the absences are nefariously hidden.

A History and Theory of the Line in English Language Poetry

Encountering The Poetic Line In English

For me, and for generations of US readers before me, poetry has been defined by the appearance of the line break on the page, that ragged right-hand margin signaling that something is at work in the arrangement of the words on paper beyond mere transcription, or perhaps, the suggestion that transcription might itself be a form of choreography. In my childhood homes, only books offered me privacy. If I played the piano, practiced ballet, watched a VHS tape, or played a record, the sounds and sights were impossible to hide. Books put me out of reach, hidden in plain sight. The act of reading felt like a cloak of invisibility—though this may have had less to do with reading itself than my mother's belief that readers must be left in peace to read. Reading was an initiation. I was being initiated into print culture—which felt universal and timeless—but is in fact contingent and historical. As a reader, I found that poetry felt more intimate than prose, the voice in my head guided by lineation in ways that I've spent a lifetime trying to understand.

There are three paradoxes at the heart of print culture: 1) reading on the page demands a kind of introverted extroversion, or extroverted introversion; 2) reading on the page offers the sounds of silent voices, heard in one's head, and the specificity of each voice is what we often call "style"; 3) reading on the page offers profound intimacy with complete strangers, and quite often these strangers are dead.

Literacy is a late development among humans, and no one has better explored what it means to transition from an oral culture to a literate culture than Anne Carson. In *Eros the Bittersweet*, Carson writes, "An individual who lives in an oral culture uses his senses differently than one who lives in a literate culture, and with that different sensual deployment comes a different way of conceiving his own relations with his environment, a different conception of his body and a different conception of his self" (43). Literacy requires a kind of retreat from the world, a closing off. For the person in an oral culture, "Complete openness to the environment is a condition of optimum awareness and alertness" (43–44), but "as an individual reads and writes he gradually learns to close or inhibit the input of his senses" (44). Carson notes that this leads to an erotic loss, and her observation of how the poets experience their newfound literacy sounds very much like Jacques Lacan's theory of the mirror stage, the stage in which a child sees itself in the mirror and understands that it is isolated from, rather than continuous with, its caregiver. "The poets record this struggle from within a consciousness—perhaps new in the world—of the body as a unity of limbs, senses and self, amazed at its own vulnerability" (45). Clearly, my childhood experience of discovering reading closely tracks society's experience—ontogeny recapitulating phylogeny.

My interest is in how poetry retains that sense of the oral, in how to understand the symbiosis of the spoken voice and written record. The poetic line would seem to be a product of writing, and yet the truth is that writing makes manifest or literal a concept that had previously been an abstraction.

That the poetic line predates its now-familiar version on the page is suggested by the etymology of the word "verse." To quote *The New Princeton Encyclopedia of Poetry and Poetics*: "'Verse,' we may recall, etymologically harkens back to the Latin 'versus' meaning 'turn,' namely the turn at the end of the line.. v[erse] is therefore lang[uage] (1) given rhythmical order and (2) set into lines" (1348). In its Latin roots, the turning suggested by "verse" is the turning of a plow (also suggested by "fers" in Old English) and the lines that result from the plow moving to one side of the field and back again, like the lawnmower leaving stripes on a football field. However, this metaphor (where poetry's lines are the tenor, and furrows in the earth are the vehicle) breaks down under close examination. In the first place, every line of a rectangular field is the same length; not so lines of poetry, at least as far back as sapphic stanzas. In the second place, in plowing, the plow does not magically return to the left side of the field and then proceed to the right side of the field, in the way that English writing leaps back to the left side of the page. Like the lawn-mower, the plow goes from one side to the other and then back again. A form of writing that goes from one side of the page to the other and back again in this manner does exist—it's called a boustrophedon—and boustrophedonic writing in Greek predates the writing of Greek consistently from left to right. In Greek tragedy, the strophe and the antistrophe were corresponding metrical units performed by the chorus, with the epode concluding the trio of lines. According to the *Princeton Encyclopedia*, the strophe was performed while turning toward the altar, and the antistrophe was performed while counter-turning away, followed by a stationary epode (1215). According to *Britannica*, the strophe was performed by the chorus while moving left to right and the antistrophe was performed while moving right to left—a boustrophedonic choreography of the poetic line literalized in the bodies of actors.

"Poetry" is a more capacious category than "verse," and a later entrant into the English language. "Verse"—meaning "a succession of words arranged according to natural or recognized rules of prosody and forming a complete metrical line; one of the lines of a poem or piece of versification"—was first recorded, according to the *Oxford English Dictionary*, around 900 CE, while "poetry"—child of "poesis," meaning "made thing"—did not enter English until the late 1300s.

When thinking about the line, I find it hard to separate my own idea of poetry from my own idea of verse—or rather, even though I know that not all poetry is lineated, I tend to discuss poetry as though it were defined by lineation. Since modernism, the category "Poetry" has contained pretty much everything that isn't clearly another genre. While rhythm, rhyme, and meter—the classic markers of "Verse"—haven't gone anywhere, they do go in and out of style. "Doggerel" is quite clearly verse, and yet one would be hard-pressed to find a faculty member at an MFA program in the United States (or an editor at a serious literary journal) who would admit to valuing doggerel as poetry, even though "deadline poet" Calvin Trillin continues to publish his political light verse[1] in *The Nation*. Keeping doggerel at bay might even be precisely the exclusion that makes capital-P-poetry a big tent, making room for sonnets composed entirely of lipstick colors, letters gridded out to spell a single word over and over as it intersects with itself, or even asemic writing that looks like it should be readable, but is not. Our current conception of poetry gives it the power to overlap or consume: the "memoir in verse" and the "novel in verse" remain popular—though in hybridity, the lineation of verse often reasserts itself as the primary quality of poetry. As the old joke goes, everything aspires to be "poetic," except poetry; describing poetry as "poetic" is an insult.

A Flawed but Useful Attempt to Isolate the Essence of Poetry

Are poetry and prose mutually exclusive? If yes, the Venn diagram between them might look like this:

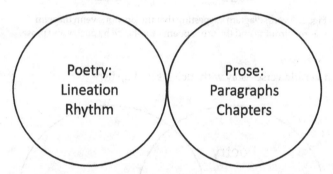

Fig01: A venn diagram playfully suggesting that prose and poetry can be theorized as having no overlap.

Both poetry and prose share the sentence as an organizing unit, and both would share the book as a unit of distribution, so already my diagram is flawed, but for the vast majority of writing, the above diagram could be sufficient if we wanted there to be no overlap. But at the very least, we should acknowledge the prose poem. If we add the prose poem to our taxonomy, we get something like this:

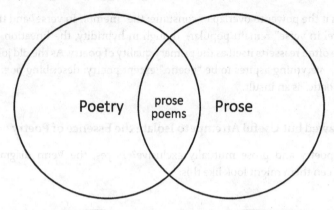

Figo2: A venn diagram suggesting that the previous venn diagram
was too limiting and the prose poems are shared by poetry and prose.

And if we add verse—stay with me—we end up here:

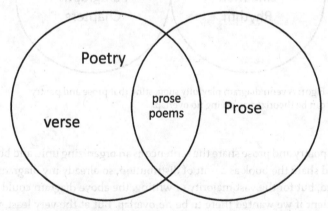

Figo3: A venn diagram suggesting that the previous venn diagram
could include verse as a subset of poetry, but that would not at all
overlap with prose poems.

And if we added lineated poetry we begin to reach the upper end of the
Venn diagram's use:

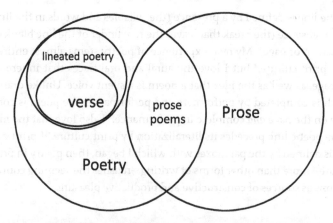

Fig04: A venn diagram suggesting that the previous venn diagram could include verse as a subset not only of poetry, but as a subset of lineated poetry, which itself is a subset of poetry.

Or we might go back to the previous diagram and simply shade everything that is not prose poetry as lineated poetry, though we might need carve-outs for visual poetry, concrete poetry, erasure poetry, and poetry that is neither lineated nor in prose blocks. And where drama would fit, I have no idea, though my best guess is "everywhere."

I know that this is a lot of Venn diagrams, and it might seem like an odd way into a discussion of the poetic line in English, but I wanted to start here for two reasons. The first is that I wanted to explore where exactly the poetic line falls in our current conceptions of writing, before sliding back to the origins of writing, and looking at how what we now know as the poetic line came to be the line we recognize when flipping through an anthology or opening our Poem-a-Day email from the Academy of American Poets. The second is that I wanted a visual illustration of how quickly genre distinctions can border on the absurd when too much effort is made to police those boundaries. Any good deconstructionist is suspicious of binaries and divisions, but unless we have a shared idea of what the poetic line *is*, any discussion of the line will be incoherent— even though most of the fun usually lies in the limit cases and outliers, not the broad swath of *mostly-the-case*. Though without a clear sense of what's *mostly-the-case*, how would one recognize outliers and limit cases as such?

The line is defined by a presence (the syllables and words in the line) and an absence (the break that leaves the remainder of the line blank on the screen or page). My own experience of poetry stems almost entirely from print culture,[2] but I love the aural and oral traces that inhere on the page, as well as the idea that a poem is a silent voice. Unlike drama, which is completed by performers and performance, the poem is complete on the page *and* complete in performance.[3] I also love that the idea of the poetic line precedes its literalization by print culture. If print culture is defined by the paradoxes with which I began, then poetry in print culture—more than other forms of writing—relishes the seeming contradictions as sources of constructive and productive pleasure.

A Partial and Messy Genealogy of the Written Line of Poetry in English

The line break is a form of punctuation. To say that the line ending is a form of punctuation is to say that the line break is a symbol that clarifies meaning for the reader. M. B. Parkes, in his book-length study *Pause and Effect: An Introduction to the History of Punctuation in the West*, explains that punctuation's "primary function is to resolve structural uncertainties in a text, and to signal nuances of semantic significance which might otherwise not be conveyed at all, or would at best be much more difficult for a reader to figure out" (1). The visual features that define the line on the page are not an instruction to make a particular sound (as the letter "b" might be an instruction to make a "b" sound), but rather a guide to the choreography of the sounds indicated by the letters in the words (despite the English language's awkward relationship to phonetics). The gap of space that runs to the right margin of the page, the indentation of a line's beginning, and the blank space of a stanza break are all—like periods and commas and quotations marks—part of the apparatus that makes sense of how those words are intended to be understood in relation to each other. However, the line as we recognize it now is not the only way that the line has been understood or transcribed historically.

Parkes writes: "The fundamental principle for interpreting punctuation is that the value and function of the symbol must be assessed in relation to other symbols in the immediate context, rather than in relationship to a supposed absolute value and function for the symbol when considered in isolation" (2). Bearing this in mind, neither the line nor the line break can ever be a unitary device; they are mutually constructed parts of a multifaceted form of annotation, constantly in relationship to what has come before and what is happening in the moment, as the reader's eyes traverse the page. Our current system of punctuation asks most of our punctuation marks to do more than one thing: periods can end sentences or indicate abbreviation; semicolons can join independent clauses or separate items in a list; apostrophes can show possession or omission. It should be no surprise that the line break (or the line ending) is asked to do multiple kinds of work.

Composing poetry would seem to be a universal human instinct, even if there is no world-historical agreement on what poetry is or how it should be represented in writing (or more accurately: how it should be visually represented). That my own conception of poetry is so completely linked with writing is a result of technological developments and historical events. The archeological work of Denise Schmandt-Besserat has shown that the history that the West had imagined (or had speculated) for writing was usually quite wrong, and often even backwards. Writing developed independently in three areas of the world: China, Mesoamerica, and Mesopotamia (Schmandt-Besserat, 1). Users of written English can trace their writing system back to Mesopotamian tokens used for record keeping and accounting (7). These tokens were stored in opaque clay containers, and the tokens were impressed into the wet clay to show what was inside the opaque clay envelope, though at some point, it became clear to the token counters that the impressions on the surface of the clay could replace the tokens inside the clay envelopes (7). The tokens from which writing emerged were not representative, but abstract (7). Schmandt-Besserat explains that "counting was not, as formerly assumed, subservient to writing; on the contrary, writing emerged from counting" (8). We imagine that a return to the mimetic is primitive, but current conceptions of writing's history place abstraction at the origin point. The impressions on the clay looked like the tokens that had been impressed, but the tokens looked nothing like what they were intended to track (7). A jar of oil was represented by an ovoid token, not a jug-shaped token (7). There is a certain irony in the fact that the first writing was actually a mimetic representation of an abstraction: the ovoid impression looks like the ovoid token; the ovoid token looks nothing like a jar of oil.

Abstraction preceded the pictographic, despite the pictographic *seeming* like a more obvious first step. More precisely, the figurative nature of the token gave birth to the pictographic representation of the token.

Barry Powell picks up the story of writing in his *Writing: Theory and History of the Technology of Civilization.* Those pictographic markings impressed into the clay envelopes developed into "logograms"—or picture words that provided a kind of rebus. The first alphabet, in which letters represented consonant sounds, was developed in roughly 1500 BC in what is now Lebanon. This alphabet developed over time, and in roughly 800 BC, the Greeks added letters to represent vowel sounds, giving a newfound clarity to the phonetic aspect of writing. While it's often said that many Eastern forms of writing are pictographic rather than phonetic, the truth is that phonetic and pictographic features often work in tandem. Even though we consider English phonetic, letters often make very different sounds (the "c" in "car"; the "c" in "centile"; the "c" in "ciabatta"), and we might consider that adoption of the emoji has reintroduced pictographic features to English in past decades. If I type a colon and a parenthesis in Microsoft Word, it is now *autocorrected* to a smiley face. With no effort on my part, ":)" becomes " ☺ ".

The Greeks' introduction of letters to represent vowel sounds clarified an ambiguity present in previous writing systems. In ancient Greece, writing was primarily used for the transcription of speeches (Parkes, 9). Oration stood out as the mark of the learned, and speechmaking was the primary goal of education (9). This practice continued in Rome, where the Latin letters we still use today got their start. Texts were largely written in *scriptio continua* (10), meaning that there were none of the punctuation marks or visual arrangements that we expect to help us make sense of a text, and reading a text without extensive preparation would be something akin to our experience of sight reading a musical score at a piano.[4] Some people are good at it, but most of us are not. Parkes recounts a phrase from the *Aeneid,* "collectamexiliopubem," that could be read "collectam exilio pubem" ("a people gathered for exile") or "collectam ex Ilio pubem" ("a people gathered from Troy") in order to illustrate the ambiguities of scriptio continua (10). But while this form of writing seems to us like the sort of thing that ought not last a thousand years—our modern eyes see this as a problem to be fixed, not an ambiguity to be reckoned with— Parkes clarifies that the value of scriptio continua was that the reader had a "neutral text" (11) for preparation. The ambiguity was a feature, not a bug. During this time, what we now know as punctuation was inserted by the reader, and the first form of punctuation was simply a dot inserted between words to clarify the words' boundaries.[5] Imagine, for a moment: a highly anticipated book of poems arrived to you with just letters filling the entire page, and you get to insert all of the punctuation and line breaks yourself. Or imagine that helping your children with their homework consistedofhelpingyourchildrenfindwherethedotsgobetweenthewords.

In researching the history of writing, I have been struck by how many echoes across time are created by technology. The ambiguities of scriptio continua, having disappeared for centuries, returned with URLs. A website to find agents for entertainers is called "Who Represents," but "whorepresents.com" could also look like a site for sex workers reclaiming a slur.

Verse in the ancient world was set in lines, rather than scriptio continua (97). The lines were aligned to the left margin or indented to indicate different meters or measures (97). So in a sapphic stanza, the first three hendecasyllabic lines would be against the left margin, and the forth adonic line would be indented. First letters of each line were capitalized (*litterae notabiliories*) and separated from the rest of the line by a large space, though shorter poems were centered (98).

Old English was not transcribed using Latin letters until the Anglo-Saxons were converted to Christianity (Bright, 16), which began in 597, when Augustine of Canterbury converted the Kentish King Æðelberht (109). A runic alphabet known as *fuþark* was established in Britain by the late 600s (Findell, 24), and over the following two centuries, the runic alphabet was expanded into what we now call *futhork* (35). Both futhark and furthork are named for the first six letters of the alphabet (sadly, we can't form a pronounceable word from "ABCDEF," though we do encourage children to learn their "ABCs"). Futhork and Latin letters were often used together for space in inscriptions (38), though Latin letters won out in the end, as runes were used for "brief transcriptions of a magical, monumental or practical nature" rather than for longer works (Bright, 16). Futharc was most likely adapted from the Etruscan or Phoenician alphabet (Van Gelderen, 54).

New letters were introduced to represent Old English sounds that were not in the Latin tongue. Two letters were borrowed from runes: "þ" (a "th" sound) and "Þ" (a "w" sound). The letters "ð" (a "th" sound) and "æ" (a short "a" sound as in "bat" or "ash") were adapted from Latin letters (Bright, 16). (The "Ye" in old-timey titles like "Ye olde apothecary" is actually pronounced "The" and the not-actually-a-"y" in "ye" is a stylized "þ"). The "ȝ" or "yogh" made a "gh" or "ch" sound (as in "Bach" or "chutzpah") and a few other sounds. Interestingly, none of the letters added to Latin for Old English have survived into Modern English, though "w" and "j" are newer additions that have persisted.

Manuscript culture preceded print culture, and those manuscripts reflect the conditions of the page, though a page that was produced by hand. The only extant version of the Old English poem *Beowulf*, dated to roughly the eleventh century, is not lineated in the modern sense, but is also not scriptio continua. There are spaces between words, section breaks, initial capitals, and *puncta* (or dots) to mark the line breaks. The features of poetry in the manuscript tradition were often quite playful to print-accustomed eyes. Parkes reproduces this poem, which uses a combination of virgules and periods, as an example of the "punctuation poems" that began being written in the 1400 and 1500s (107):[6]

Trusty . seldom / to their ffrendys uniust . /
Gladd for to help . no crysten creator /
Wyllyng to greve . setting all þeir ioy and lust
Only in þee pleasour of God . having no cure /
Who is most ryche . with them þeey wylbe sewer /
Wher need is . gevyng neyther reward ne ffee /
Vnresonably . Thus leve prestys parde. /

If you read with the virgules, you get

Trusty seldom.
To their friends unjust.
Glad to help no Christian Creator.
Willing to hurt,
Setting all their joy and desire in the pleasure of God having no cure.
Who is most riche, with them they will surely be.
Where need is, they give neither reward nor fee.
Unreasonably, thus live priests, by God!

But if you parse the syntax based on periods, you get

Trusty.
Seldom to their friends unjust.
Glad to help.
No Christian creator are they willing to pain.
They set all their joy and desire in the pleasure of God.
Having no cure for the wealthy,
They will be sure to be where need is.
Giving neither reward nor fee unreasonably.
Thus live priests, by God!

Essentially, you have two different poems—one celebrating the virtuous priest and one condemning the vicious priest. I've updated the language a bit, and the word "parde" can have the meaning of "by God" as both a despairing and an affirming interjection.[7] Changes in punctuation created the possibility for new forms of composition.

This "doubling" effect has been mirrored in the possibilities created by the internet. In the early 2010s, there was a vogue for "Reverse poems" or "Palindrome poems" that, when read line by line from top to bottom, were despairing and sad, but read line by line from bottom to top became hopeful and optimistic. Jonathan Reed's 2013 poem "The Lost Generation" opens, "I am part of a lost generation. / And I refuse to believe that / I can change the world," which means that it ends, "I can change the world / And I refuse to believe that / I am part of a lost generation." YouTube and accessible editing software allowed the reverse poems to be composed and distributed in a new way, just as the nascent techniques of manuscript and punctuation allowed this medieval poet to playfully inscribe two poems into one set of words. The technologies of writing necessarily influence what it is that gets written, and how it is transcribed and distributed. The line as a unit may precede writing, and yet changes in technology have the power to reinvent the line. And even if the palindrome poem was a fad, it was an impactful one. There are over seventeen million views of Jonathan Reed's poem.

As rhyme became a structuring device of medieval European poetry, rhyme was often placed after brackets (Parkes, 99). To give a sense of what this looked like using a recent example, W. H. Auden's stanza

Let us honour if we can
The vertical man,
Though we value none
But the horizontal one
　　(53)

　　might have been written as

Let us honour if we c
　　　　　　　　 ⟩ *an*
The vertical m

Though we value n
　　　　　　　　 ⟩ *one*
But the horizontal

In looking at medieval texts, we are mistaken if we assume a symmetry between our reading practices and theirs. Katharine Jager explains, "Medieval 'reading' is in fact an aural practice of recitation, memorization and listening as well as textual examination, a hybrid practice dating to the beginning of the medieval" (n. p.). The writing that survives from the medieval period is an unruly amalgam of multilingual and multimodal practice. Ardis Butterfield argues against trying to pin down poetry in the medieval period, explaining that for someone like me looking for a recognizable poetic past, "the most central challenges are to Anglocentricity, language, literariness, and print-based notions of form" (326). Butterfield considers a poem that "is a two-part motet—that is a voice part that sings the text and a second part, the tenor, which is taken from a section of chant. Motet texts have no 'norm' for the modern editor to reconstruct" (329). Twentieth century US print culture was unitary and standardized in a way that is historically anomalous. Butterfield compares the way in which Emily Dickinson's work was standardized to fit notions of "lyric" to the way that medieval texts have been misrecognized, pointing out that reproductions are often reshaped to current expectations, and that "the modern lyric came into being when readers decided they wanted to read poems *as* lyrics." If we see history as a mirror of ourselves, or as a continuous trajectory leading up to our current selves and practices, we

risk losing the strangeness (to us) of what came before and the disconti-
nuities and ruptures that have shaped the world we inhabit.

By the 1400s, the Ellesmere manuscript of Chaucer was transcribed
in lines that are recognizable to the contemporary reader as lines. By the
1500s and 1600s, printed works like *Tottel's Miscellany* and Shakespeare's
plays and poems are accessible to contemporary readers. Scribes accus-
tomed to the indentations indicated by the matching meters of Greek
and Latin poetry transferred those indicators to show stanzas or rhyme
in English poetry, such that one might find the final couplet of a sonnet
indented, or the rhyme scheme made visible through indentation. Contemporary readers can read facsimile versions of most early modern British texts with little difficulty, unlike the expertise required to engage earlier texts in English. That "Juliet" is spelled "Iuliet" or that an "f" (or an "f"
without the cross bar) is an "s" will be a fairly low barrier to entry. There
are a handful of true ambiguities in Shakespeare: in *Romeo and Juliet*,
there is simply no way to determine if the word "finne" (which occurs in
an embedded sonnet) should be transported into contemporary English
orthography as "sin" or "fine." Both words fit the sense and meter. The
handful of ambiguities in a body of work as large as Shakespeare's stand
out because of how truly unusual they are.

I had hoped to trace a genealogy of the poetic line in English, but in
truth, that hope was based on simplified trajectories of the linguistic history that I had learned as an undergraduate. Those sweeping (and linear)
histories masked the true complexity and diversity of how writing happened in the many centuries between the advent of written English and
the development of norms for writing. Butterfield again: "The stubbornly
undistinguished mass of medieval insular verse almost defies explication
and analysis. This quagmire of verse is a vast, nebulous, ill-defined area"
(327). Full of a mixture of languages, intended performance styles, and
methods of transcription, medieval verse is by no means unitary. I no
longer think that I can pinpoint precisely how the line became *the line*. I
am out of my depth as a scholar when trying to follow arguments about,
say, how to spell the name of the poet Laȝamon,[8] but as a poet, seeing
that the line has been multiply transcribed and formed gives me a sense
of freedom and possibility that makes the digital age feel anticipated,
rather than destructive.

As we move further and further into the digital age, we need an adjective that will replace "printed" or "written" when it comes to "word." The fluidity of digital writing undoes much of the permanence and stability that the technology of ink on pages has offered for millennia. In trying to access the University of Oxford's Quarto Archive, to review facsimile pages of Shakespeare, I encountered this message: "We regret to inform users that this resource is no longer available. The site has been withdrawn (or abandoned) as the technologies which it is built with have reached end-of-life." That the Quarto is still legible some five centuries after its publication, but that the Quarto archive met obsolescence within two decades of its existence, ought to underscore that the convenience of the digital is inextricably yoked to ephemerality. Digitized texts are fickle. Oni Buchanan's digital poetry project relied on Flash, which my web browser will no longer run. While books go in and out of print, purely digital texts are more like Marc Quinn's frozen blood sculptures: one lengthy power outage away from disappearing.

I may sound like a Luddite, but even as I have my suspicions, I have embraced the digital in nearly all aspects of my life as a poet, scholar, and teacher, which may be why I am so aware of the dangers it presents to the archives that future scholars will rely on. I have mostly stopped using anthologies and consult Poetryfoundation.org and Poets.org for classroom instruction; but using these resources does not leave behind a sedimented record of what was popular and when. Worse: it allows for erasure, which can be a form of justice or correction, but is also a form of historical distortion. If I am not mistaken, one of the poems representing Amiri Baraka on Poetryfoundation.org used to be "Death Is Not as Natural as You Fags Seem to Think," taken from his 1969 collection *Black Magic*. The poem is not there now, but the poem is in Baraka's collected works. If I were an anthologist, I would likely not advocate for the inclusion of that poem. I would hesitate to teach it in a class. But I kept returning to it in part because I just couldn't believe that it was real. I also like the poem (which I don't understand at all) and am endlessly puzzled by my implication in the poem as a gay man (or should I not center myself?). But I also know that the casual use of the word "fag" is shocking now in a way that it was not when Baraka was writing.[9] Stephen Sondheim included the lyric "I could understand a person / if a person was a fag" in the original 1970 production of *Company* as a knowing in-joke, not as a homophobic slur. I can listen to the original cast recording to confirm that my memory is accurate. But as I said, even as I see the dangers, I do not reject the digital. I consulted Baraka's collected works through the New York Public Library's online collection. I listened to the original cast recording of *Company* on Spotify.

As we move to shifting online archives like Poetryfoundation.org or OED.com, there are fewer and fewer sedimented editions that one can consult in order to confirm one's historical memory. It wouldn't surprise me at all if I were mistaken about finding that poem at Poetryfoundation. org. Maybe I was reading Baraka's poem on Poets.org or some other website; my memory has often proved to be correct in the outlines, but faulty in the details. For future scholars, when the poem was removed will be an important index of when tolerance for anti-gay slurs within literary spaces evaporated. The fact that it was present online and then removed online consigns it to a kind of black hole of archival knowledge. (Sadly, the Wayback Machine at archive.org, which is supposed to solve this problem, has never worked for me.) The kinds of plates and facsimiles I relied on to help me understand the history of writing exist because both the manuscripts and the reproductions are ink on paper or parchment. Pixels have their purposes, but longevity is not among them.

Having come of age in the 1990s, I was educated in a post–Cold War moment when serious people believed that we had reached a kind of pleasant world-historical stasis. Francis Fukuyama's 1992 *The End of History and the Last Man* argued that liberal democracy and capitalism were humanity's future, and that we could sort of relax into it. The internet was not initially seen in the 1990s as the harbinger of new forms of writing, but rather as a more convenient way to distribute writing as it was. I remember Amazon.com in the 1990s as nothing more than a bookstore with good prices—I certainly didn't foresee it becoming a disruptive force that would threaten the entire publishing industry. And yet now we find ourselves in the midst of a new technology that has irrevocably altered what it means to write and publish.

Aarthi Vadde's recent essay "Platform or Publisher" contains not only a critique of the social media landscape that is wreaking havoc on our democracy, but also a critique of scholars like me, whose preference for print makes them eager to avoid the impact of Web 2.0. "It will be up to legislators to hold social media companies to regulatory account, but it remains the vital task of scholars in the humanities to make collective sense of the mediascape their platforms have created" (456). Recently, while reading my Poem-a-Day email from the Academy of American Poets on my phone, I casually turned the phone from portrait to landscape, and watched as the short-lined poem I had been reading suddenly transformed into a long-lined poem. Vadde's call to action makes my example seem impossibly banal, and yet this simple device-inflected fluidity of line is imbricated in the way that technology is changing writing, and by extension, everything else.

Clearly, history did not end, and right now we are witnessing a profound change in writing. I suspect that the future of writing will not be entirely without genre (even the Amazon store puts cookbooks in a cookbook section), but the idea of specializing in a particular genre is already falling away. As every poet is told by their publisher, the way to sell your book of poems is to write and publish texts that are not poems. Younger writers will cultivate careers that look more like James Baldwin's or Oscar Wilde's than Robert Pinsky's or Louise Glück's. I think that Bob Dylan's Nobel Prize was a mistake, but it may be a harbinger of expansive boundaries in literature, even to the non-literary, or the literary-adjacent. One reason for this is that postmodernist thinking has made us suspicious of all category distinctions. Another reason for this dissolution of genre is a move toward global thinking, and internationally, many of our Western genre distinctions are either without merit or incoherent. Academia began playing patron to the literary arts in roughly the 1930s, and a focus on genre distinction for writing lined up with academia's disciplinary preference for narrow specialization. Academia was often a generous patron through much of the twentieth century, though in our current moment a panoply of factors (including declining enrollment, closing colleges, shuttered programs, and the Trump administration's alienation of international students) has eroded the share of spoils available to emerging poets.

But what does this mean for the line? Simply that it will—of necessity—change, while retaining aspects of its history. It seems quite clear to me that our relationship to the line is changing because our relationship to writing is in flux. Whatever the line has been is not precisely what the line will be, as "post-print" technologies continue to further structure our lives and our relations.

This flux invites study. When things are in flux, what will soon be taken for granted remains novel, and what has long been taken for granted makes itself visible as contingent. In the concluding passage of her call to arms, Vadde writes, "Understanding literary indistinction, strange as it may sound, is what scholars need to do to keep up with literature's changing contours and constituents within a platform-based Internet culture" (461). I agree.

Three Theories of the Poetic Line in English

To speak of a theory of the line is almost necessarily to assume a free verse line, because any discussion of a metrically determined line in formal verse would have to be a theory of meter. The commonplace that all poetry is formal, whether or not it is metrical, is a bit like the truism that all poetry is political—well, yes, but sometimes that is a useful lens and sometimes it is not. A theory of the line that cannot be applied to formal verse is really no theory at all, even if free verse gives one a fresh perspective on metrical verse. There are theories of metrical lines that would not be applicable to free verse. Annie Finch, in *The Ghost of Meter*, gives an encapsulation of three prevailing theories of meter: 1) "the theory of propriety," in which certain meters are suited to certain subjects; 2) "the iconic theory," which argues that meter is a tool to enhance or reinforce the meaning of a poem; and 3) "the frame theory," in which each metrical pattern suggests the poem's heritage and relation to all prior poems in that same metrical pattern (3). Working from Aristotle forward, Finch provides an erudite and engaging survey of these theories, before arriving at her own argument for "the metrical code," which she explains as the idea that "meter can constitute a crucial aspect of the meaning of poems written during times of metrical crisis," and can "reveal the poet's attitude toward the meter's cultural and literary connotations" (1). Finch's theory of the metrical line is worth any serious poet's attention, and I provide an overview here in order to direct the reader to her work, and in order to begin to outline how the line is meaningful in ways that have implications for poetic praxis[10].

I had initially intended to give a full overview of as many theories of the poetic line in English as I could find, but I would have needed to expand this essay into at least a book. Instead, I have chosen two theories that have been meaningful to me, and that I suspected would be unfamiliar to the reader, or at least have been unfamiliar to students whom I have engaged in conversation about the line. I also want to present these theories to show that theories of the line are not necessarily symmetrical—that they can do rather different forms of work while sharing the line as an object of study. The third theory of the line is my own, and one that I have been trying to articulate for fifteen years. My own theory of the line—that it runs interference with the intonation of the sentence—is meant to supplement rather than replace other theories of the line—and is in conversation with my entire education as a poet. I have often found this theory to be implicitly present in other theories, though I have not seen it stated in quite the formulation that I offer here. I do not pretend to be without influence, but I also believe that my theory of the line rises to the level of original contribution.

Allen Grossman's Theory of the Line in Summa Lyrica (1992)

Allen Grossman's Summa Lyrica is best approached as a sort of mystical guide to poetry. While Grossman relies on a multiplicity of philosophical, critical, and religious traditions, the idea that feels most often echoed to me is Kierkegaard's famous foundation of existential Christianity that only one man is saved, but any man can be that man. "Every man can be that one, God helping him therein—but only one attains the goal" (Kierkegaard, n. p.). Grossman often returns to the idea of a single poem in the same way that Kierkegaard returns to the idea of a single man: "In matters of poetry, everybody is *trying* to say the same thing" (215); "Hence there is always only one poem. (All versions of a poem are poems.)" (222); "A poem has the same singularity as a self. The question arises: 'Why are there many poems; Why are there more poems than one?'" (235); "One life. One poem. There is one poem written by God" (245).

If one reads unkindly, the work verges on the truistic and the nonsensical. Even with the assistance of mushrooms, I doubt I could manage to find profundity in "While I am doing this, you are doing something else" (214). Similarly, in the first section on Reading: "The poem is the destiny of the reader. The reader is the destiny of the poem" (213). Um, yes. Poets will write poems, and those poems will be read by readers. "Destiny" smacks of romanticism and mysticism, but poets do write poems, and those poems do get read. When Grossman writes that "The question of value is not a question" (229), I feel tricked. This feels like linguistic gamesmanship. "Language always means something else" (229) will certainly appeal to those inclined to strong versions of Deconstruction, but even second graders are taught not to say "something else" unless their relative pronoun has an antecedent.

In returning to Grossman's work, I found myself a bit frustrated. I'm basically a materialist, and I typically use the word "mystic" as an insult to describe writing that sounds good but has no actual meaning—by which I mean writing that lacks falsifiable claims that can be checked against evidence. However, even at my grumpiest moments of Cultural Materialism, I'm still awed by observations like "The poem achieves 'closure' only when some new cognitive element has been added to the relationship of subject and object. Terminal closure is 'something understood'" (218). Or consider section 17.1: "Metaphor is a device for reducing the unknowability of the fact by eroding its uniqueness" (248). That's brilliant. Of course, part of what I find frustrating about Grossman is that nothing is *argued*: everything is *asserted*. The *Summa Lyrica* can also be quite funny: "In a radical humanism, a tragedy becomes an event from which no one goes home" (300). The best way to approach the *Summa Lyrica* is not irascibly, but with an open heart. Wanting to know if he's right or wrong is a fool's errand. Letting his ideas flow over you as you discuss them over wine— now, that's a generative project.

Grossman dedicates two sections of *Summa Lyrica* to the line. In "Line I" he focuses on the line as a unit in relationship to the breath. In "Line II" he focuses on the relations of the lines across the poem, treating the individual line as a horizontal axis, and the accumulation of lines as you read down the page as the vertical axis of the poem, bringing a Cartesian order to the poem itself.

Grossman has two categories of breath. The "Greater or Feeding Breath" (279) is the inhale. By contrast, the "Lesser, or Dead, or Speech Breath" is the exhale (279). This makes biological sense—the inhale is the expansion of the body, the filling of the lungs with oxygenated air that carries nutrients to the bloodstream. In asthma, an attack of wheezing is life threatening because the asthmatic cannot breathe in. But for the exhale to be lesser or dead makes for an odd sense when speech, singing, or (if you play a wind instrument) blowing happen in the exhale. "Speech is obtained by *inscription* upon the dead breath, a meddling with the exhausted air as it is pushed from the body outward" (279). The line is happening in coordination with the lesser breath—the gaps between the lines infuse the speaking body with life, while the spoken line itself is a form of death. In this division, silence is a form of health, while oral communication is a form of decay.

Grossman's taxonomy of the line has to do with the ten-syllable line as the base unit. "The line of ten floats in a social space managing its boundedness by stratagems of reciprocity" (280). In the ten-syllable line, "persons address one another in human scale" (280), and Grossman compares the speaking persona to a character in a drama—fully formed, fully realized, fully human. The line of less than ten syllables is a bit more mysterious. This shorter line is where "transformations occur." There's an almost echo-chamber-like silence that attends the shorter-than-ten-syllable line: "Alternative versions of the same utterance are very remote; not even a faint murmuring is heard" (280). The social space of ten syllables is reduced to an isolation chamber, the reverberation of internality. In the greater-than-ten-syllable line, "the speaker in the poem bleeds outward as in trance or sleep toward other states of himself" (280). The ten-syllable line brings the speaker past his human boundaries, and enters ecstatic forms of communication wherein the speaking self expands past the expected limitations.

This theory of the line finds mysticism on either side of the ten-syllable line. At less than ten lies monastic meditation, a fall into a kind of silence that leaves one alone with oneself. At greater than ten, we find the prophetic voice, spoken by the inhabited visionary who speaks on behalf of something larger than himself. In both cases, slipping away from the pentameter results in something not precisely unworldly, but something uncanny, or at least something that tears the fabric of the quotidian. This theory is stunningly useful in that allows the writer to consider how the voice is to be constructed.[11]

It is also the case that while Grossman's theory is not *scientific* in that it makes significant claims that are not falsifiable, I have consistently found it to be true. Interestingly, Grossman's claims are increasingly supported by neuroscience research on reading. Grossman discusses how the line moves from possibility to actuality. He describes the line as "moving from less differentiation and more possibility toward more differentiation and less possibility" (281). This matches Maryanne Wolf's description of the neuroscience of reading almost exactly—that the brain filters through what the words might mean before settling on what they do mean.

Ellen Louise Hart and Martha Nell Smith

For a queer theory of the poetic line in English, one needs look no further than Ellen Louise Hart and Martha Nell Smith's highly influential study of Emily Dickinson, *Open Me Carefully*. In returning to Dickinson's fascicles, Hart and Smith emphasize the material quality of the manuscripts. "All of Dickinson's letters and poems are handwritten, and certain manuscript features—calligraphic orthography, punctuation, capitalization, and line breaks—help to convey meaning" (xxiii). Starting with transcriptions of Homer, lineation has been a way to capture the metrical qualities of the language in poetry. The half-joke/half-truth that you can sing Emily Dickinson poems to "The Yellow Rose of Texas" or the *Gilligan's Island* theme song comes out of the way that her poems can be written out as alternating lines of iambic tetrameter and iambic trimeter. But Hart and Smith insist that this is wrong, that "Dickinson used the page itself, and the placement of words in relation to embossments, attachments, and margins to convey meaning, and in ways that typography cannot sufficiently transmit" (xxiii). In other words, to treat the metrical units of Dickinson's poetry as the truth of her line is misleading. The main argument of Hart and Smith is that by regularizing the manuscripts to fit print culture, what gets lost is Emily's passionate, physical, and likely consummated love for her sister-in-law Susan Dickinson. A good century of heterosexist scholars might have seen no more than obtuse metaphor in "Rowing in Eden— / Ah—the Sea! / Might I but moor—Tonight / —In thee" (9–12), while Hart and Smith find the physicality. Cardi B and Megan Thee Stallion might be better guides to Dickinson's image than the New Critics.

Emily Dickinson died in 1886, and her poems were first printed in a collection in 1890 (xvi). The basic outline of the Dickinson family love pentagon: Emily Dickinson had a passionate friendship with Susan Gilbert beginning in the 1850s. Susan Gilbert married Emily's brother Austin in 1856, becoming Susan Dickinson, and Emily's sister-in-law. Emily and Austin had a third sibling named Lavinia, commonly called Vinnie. The 1890 collection was Vinnie's idea, and she assigned the editorial task to Susan, to whom many of the poems had been written, sometimes embedded in letters. Susan wanted "to showcase the entire range of Emily's writings: letters, humorous writings, illustrations" (xvi). Vinnie wanted only a collection of poems, and feeling that Susan was taking too long, Vinnie reassigned the task to Mabel Loomis Todd, who was also Austin Dickinson's lover. *Poems by Emily Dickinson*, edited by Mabel Loomis Todd, appeared in 1890. Thomas Wentworth Higginson's introduction to this collection established the myth of the "recluse of Amherst." Mabel Loomis Todd—who never actually met Emily—also edited *Letters of Emily Dickinson*, which appeared in 1894, and effectively removed any mention of Susan from the poems. Susan herself destroyed letters that were "too personal and adulatory ever to be printed" (Dickinson quoted in Hart & Smith, xxii), leaving an even less complete record to history.

Consider this poem by Dickinson in the conventional lineation, numbered 816 in R. W. Franklin's edition:

816

I could not drink it, Sweet,
Till You had tasted first,
Though cooler than Water was
The Thoughtfulness of Thirst.

and the version Hart and Smith present as 101:

101

I could not drink
it, Sue,
Till you had tasted
first—
Though cooler than
the Water—was
The Thoughtfulness of
Thirst,
   EMILY.

Certainly, the eroticism is present in the names—the direct address of Sue, the signature, "Emily"—and Dickinson often signed her poems "Emily" or "Emilie" when sending drafts to Sue—but it is also there in the lineation, the pulsing of the longer and shorter lines, the sharp breaks against syntax and the pauses. In considering Emily as writing about queer desire, there are some poems that need little more than to not be read with the assumption that all writers are straight; but other poems reflect some anxiety about the directness of the expression. Like her rough contemporary Walt Whitman, Dickinson did change the gender of pronouns in poems to create heterosexual narratives where queer ones had existed in previous versions. Hart and Smith note that in one draft of "I showed her Hights / she never saw—," a poem that ends with a potential lover unable to reciprocate desire, there is a later version reading "He showed me Hights I / never saw—" (117). At the end of the 1800s, homosexuality was seen as stain in need of cleaning, and as Dickinson's work began being published, the eroticism was wiped away. In erasing Sue from Emily's poems, Mabel had erased her lover's wife as well as Emily's eroticism. In 1998, Hart and Smith revolutionized the way that Dickinson and her work were seen. Restoring Dickinson's original line breaks radically revised the way we understand Dickinson's work and life.

A New Theory of Intonational Interference

I offer my own contribution, not as a replacement to other theories of the line, but rather as a supplement. Put simply, my theory is this: The line runs interference with the intonation of the sentence.

Beginnings and endings—in art and language—are always stressed positions. This, I believe, is axiomatic. I greatly prefer two- or three-act plays to one-act plays because of the intermission. There is a different rhythm to a play with intermissions than to a play without intermissions. The curtain drop and sudden darkness that mark the end of the act (followed by the slow rise of the house lights) punctuate the play and give stress to whatever precedes the end of the act. Similarly, the beginning of the next act has an added emphasis. These curtain drops are not unlike the line break, section break, or chapter ending. Rhythm is not simply something that fills the duration of any given piece, but rather the result of starting and stopping—the silences on either side. In a written poem, the beginning and ending of each line are slightly stressed positions, having a weight that is often so light as to be unnoticed, but ineluctably present.

Most poets are familiar with the notation for stress and meter—the ˘ / | ˘ / | ˘ / | ˘ / | ˘ / of iambic pentameter—though it has become a common convention to put stressed syllables in bold type, rather than running the "˘" and "/" across the top of the line, with vertical lines to divide feet. But in the same way that rhythm is frequently what creates the pleasures of rhyme, sentence intonation is a significant part of the pleasures of rhythm. In the same way that rhythm is usually reduced to two basic building blocks (stressed and unstressed syllables), sentence intonation is often marked with two basic building blocks, rising pitch and falling pitch. In both cases, the reality of the rhythm, meter, and intonation are far more complex. However, I will use a notation designed to be practical, and instructive: a notation for the generalist, not the specialist.

A rising arrow (↗) prior to the word indicates a rising pitch, as associated with a question, and a falling arrow (↘) prior to the word indicates a falling pitch, as associated with closure. This is somewhat crude—suggesting rising and falling as the only options for English pitch—but I will point out that it is no more crude than the stress/unstressed dichotomy of scansion, and it has allowed me to make an argument that I have long been trying to make visible about English language poetry. While there are many sources on rising and falling intonation, I took this particular notation of the arrows from an easily accessible online source called "Learn English Today," designed to make the structures of English clear to non-native speakers. Consider the sentence, "Does he go by Joe or Joey?" There are two basic ways to say this sentence. The first would be annotated:

Does he go by ↗ Joe or ↘ Joey?

A rising pitch on the first option and a falling pitch on the second option indicates that the speaker knows that one of these two options is correct. There are no other possibilities. This is the intonation used to offer coffee or tea when those are the only drinks available. But,

Does he go by ↗ Joe or ↗ Joey?

indicates that there may be other forms of address that this Joseph prefers. As a general rule, rising pitch indicates continuation, while falling pitch indicates closure. It makes sense that a rise and fall show a complete set of options, while two rising pitches would retain a sense of openness. A fairly common form of intonation in English is the use of "↗ yes" to indicate that you would like to person who is talking to continue and that you agree, while "↘ yes" indicates that you agree and would now like to talk yourself. There are numerous ways in which intonation can impact meaning. That same rising and falling intonation can indicate hesitancy. If asked how you liked a movie,

The ↘ costumes were ↘ great!

would suggest a wholehearted endorsement of the film starting with what the actors wore. But,

The ↗ costumes were ↘ great

would indicate that everything else was pretty bad, and that the speaker will shortly explain all the awful things in the film that the sumptuous outfits could not rescue. The key to annotating pitch is to follow the voice as it is. In the same way that "tiger" is a trochee because that's how you already say it, this notation of pitch describes how we already communicate.

Within sentence intonation, falling pitch also tends to suggest where the critical information is to be found. For example, the sentence "I love dogs" would seem to have three equal stresses, but the sentence intonation will vary based on context, and the stress may shift accordingly. If asked, "Do you hate dogs?" you might respond:

I ↘ love dogs!

But if asked, "What is that you love?" your response might be:

I love ↘ dogs!

And if the question were "Who loves dogs?" the response might be:

↘ I love dogs!

Sentence intonation, obviously, is much more complex that these two crude indicators might suggest, but one of the things that we mean when we talk about "good style" in writing or "voice on the page" is writing in such a way that sentence intonation is clear. Many phrases are ambiguous in meaning and rely on the speaker's voice to give them clarity—think of the many intonations given to your name during childhood—the way your name was said when you were being praised and the way your name was said when you were in trouble. At the doctor's office, the receptionist will often call me with a rising pitch—making my name a question about my presence. Your name may always have the same stress pattern ("Jason" will always be a trochee), but the pitch varies dramatically based on the context in which your name is being said and by whom.

I think, at this point, I have sufficiently illustrated how this pitch notation might be used to reveal the intonation of the sentence, and I'd like to move on to poems. Let's start with Ada Limón's now famous poem "State Bird."

STATE BIRD

Confession: I did not want to live here,
not among the goldenrod, wild onions,
or the dropseed, not waist high in the barrel-
aged brown corn water, not with the million-
dollar racehorses, or the tightly wound
round hay bales. Not even in the old tobacco
weigh station we live in, with its heavy metal
safe doors that frame our bricked bedroom
like the mouth of a strange beast yawning
to suck us in, each night, like air. I denied it,
this new land. But, love, I'll concede this:
whatever state you are, I'll be that state's bird,
the loud, obvious blur of song people point to
when they wonder where it is you've gone.

If we were speaking this poem as prose, we would notice there are a good number of lists, which require specific rising and falling intonations:

↘ Confession: I did ↗ not want to live ↘ here, not among the ↗ goldenrod, wild ↗ onions, or the ↘ dropseed, ↗ not waist high in the barrel-aged brown corn ↘ water, ↗ not with the million-dollar ↘ racehorses, ↗ or the tightly wound round hay ↘ bales. ↗ Not even in the old tobacco weigh station we live ↘ in, ↗ with its heavy metal safe doors that frame our bricked bedroom like the mouth of a strange beast yawning to suck us in, each ↘ night, like ↘ air. I ↗ denied it, this new land. ↗ But, ↘ love, I'll concede ↘ this: ↗ whatever state you ↘ are, ↗ I'll be that state's ↘ bird, the ↗ loud, ↗ obvious blur of song people ↘ point to when they ↗ wonder where it is you've ↘ gone.

Note that the first line has precisely the same intonation that we would encounter in prose:

↘ Confession: I did ↗ not want to live ↘ here,

Both the start and the end of the line are weighted by falling pitch. The line emphasizes the natural intonation of the syntactic unit, but as the poem continues, the line ending begins to add falling pitches that were otherwise not there:

↘ not among the ↗ goldenrod, wild ↘ onions,
or the ↘ dropseed, ↗ not waist high in the ↘ barrel-
aged brown corn ↘ water, ↗ not with the ↘ million-
↘ dollar ↘ racehorses, ↘ or the tightly ↘ wound
↘ round hay ↘ bales. ↗ Not even in the old ↘ tobacco
↘ weigh ↘ station we live ↘ in, ↗ with its heavy ↘ metal
↘ safe doors that frame our bricked ↘ bedroom

I am arguing that the beginning and end of the line are weighted positions not merely in terms of stress, but also in terms of pitch. Many poets have argued this, though typically by considering the pause at the end of the line, rather than considering the emphasis given to each line's final word by that pause. It may also be the emphasis on line endings that creates the pause, and not the other way around. I am intuiting the pitches, but note that once "million" receives a falling pitch, so too must "dollar" and "racehorses." "Million" initially appears as a noun, but as it becomes an adverb, modifying "dollar," which in turn becomes an adjective modifying "racehorses," it is reduced in syntactic importance, and its subordination forces emphasis to the word it modifies and then the word that one modifies in turn. This happens precisely because "million" is at the end of the line. The exact same syntactic pattern repeats with "tobacco," as its end-of-the-line heft forces the same emphasis of a falling pitch onto "weigh" and then "station." The line pushes back against the intonation, creating additional emphasis and revising the intonation from what it would have been in prose.

like the mouth of a strange beast ↘ yawning
to suck us in, each ↘ night, like ↘ air. I ↘ denied ↘ it,
this ↘ new ↘ land. ↗ But, ↘ love, I'll concede ↘ this:
↘ whatever state you ↘ are, ↗ I'll be that state's ↘ bird,
the ↘ loud, ↘ obvious blur of song people ↘ point ↘ to
when they ↘ wonder where it is you've ↘ gone.

As the poem reaches its conclusion, the syntax begins to line up more regularly with the line ending, adding and emphasizing fall pitches. What I cannot explain is why so many words flip from a rising to a falling intonation: "loud," "obvious," and "wonder" switch pitches. This may be the origin of what is commonly known as "poetry voice"—the switching of pitch—but in this case the final effect is exquisite. The line revises the intonation of the sentence to weave in emphasis, which slows the tempo of the words, and creates the final, perfect chime of the final line.

I think that the impact of my theory will be most obvious with short-lined poems that parse the syntax. If we return to the Dickinson poem that Hart and Smith considered, the prose version would look like this:

↗ I could not drink it, ↘ Sweet, Till ↗ You had tasted ↘ first, Though ↗ cooler than ↘ Water was The ↗ Thoughtfulness of ↘ Thirst.

And in the more standardized lineation, we see a sing-song pattern encoded by the annotation: each line opens with a rising pitch and closes with a falling pitch. Along with an over-regularizing of her iambic trimeter, this lineation encourages an intonation that distracts from the meaning of the poem and foregrounds the repetitions of stress and intonation:

↗ I could not drink it, ↘ Sweet,
↗ Till You had tasted ↘ first,
Though ↗ cooler than ↘ Water was
The ↗ Thoughtfulness of ↘ Thirst.

But consider the version that Hart and Smith present with Dickinson's original:

101

I ↘ could not ↘ drink
it, ↘ Sue,
Till ↘ you had ↘ tasted
↘ first—
Though ↘ cooler than
the ↘ Water—was
The ↘ Thoughtfulness of
↘ Thirst,

    ↘ EMILY.

To me, the shorter line, and the emphasis created in the endings, reverses every rising pitch into a falling one. The sensuality of the poem lies in the way the line runs interference with the intonation of the sentence, making each stressed word a staccato stroke, rather than robbing the poem of its eroticism with a line that subordinates the sense of the words to the regularity of the way in which they are heard.

I want to consider one more poem, this one with longer sentences and longer lines. Jennifer L. Knox's "The Decorative Airport Fern Is Not What It Pretends to Be" is a kind of fever dream or surrealist experiment, in which the unreliable narrator's soliloquy reels out long syntactic units with a chatty and friendly intimacy at odds with the paranoid fantasy of sentient and communicative plants. Knox's disorienting genius carries us across her work, and she vivifies the speaker by letting the line run interference with intonation.

THE DECORATIVE AIRPORT FERN IS NOT WHAT IT PRETENDS TO BE

and it takes me a triple-take to realize it's scanning
me, or something near my ear—that must be it. No plant's
ever complimented my perfume—wait—there it goes
again. Did you see that? [Time passes, drinks] "Sure, I
remember when I thought you were a fern but you were!
Who could blame me?" I tell the what's now a magnificent
purple tetrahedron, eggplant-sized cilia straining at its corners, just
a hint of ferniness remains in its fingertips—enough to blush.
We hug goodbye. The scent of flowers lingers around me
the next day. Flying home, a decorative airport fern that really
is a decorative airport fern says, "You smell nice." I don't
believe it, but it's still a happy
ending.

As I read this poem, the longer lines and the longer sentences create fewer rises and falls in pitch than in the poems previously considered, leading to a more even pitch. If we write it out as prose, I would analyze it this way:

The decorative airport fern is ↗ not what it pretends to ↘ be and it takes me a triple-take to realize it's ↗ scanning me, or something near my ↘ ear—that must be ↘ it. No plant's ever complimented my ↘ perfume— wait—there it goes ↘ again. Did you see ↗ that? [↘ Time passes, ↘ drinks] "Sure, ↗ I remember when I thought you were a fern but you ↗ were! ↗ Who could ↘ blame me?" I tell the what's now a magnificent purple tet-rahedron, eggplant-sized cilia straining at its corners, just a hint of fern-iness remains in its fingertips—enough to ↘ blush. We hug ↘ goodbye. The scent of ↘ flowers lingers around me the next ↘ day. Flying ↗ home, a decorative airport fern that really is a decorative airport fern ↘ says, "You smell ↘ nice." I don't ↗ believe it, but it's ↗ still a happy ↘ ending.

Knox uses the title as the first line, or rather, she runs the title in to the first line syntactically. Like Limón, Knox makes the first line consistent with an unlineated syntax, though Knox places that first line in the title—

The decorative airport fern is ↗ not what it pretends to ↘ be
↗ and it takes me a triple-take to realize it's ↘ scanning
↘ me, or something near my ↘ ear—that must be ↘ it. No ↘ plant's

—but almost immediately the line breaks across syntax begin to add falling pitches, particularly to the beginning of the line. Knox is especially
adept at breaking where prose would essentially present a single syntactic unit—"scanning me," "goes again"—and splitting the words apart to
give both of them more weight.

ever complimented my ↘ perfume—wait—there it ↘ goes
↘ again. Did you see ↗ that? [↘ Time passes, ↘ drinks] "Sure, ↘ I
↘ remember when I ↘ thought you were a fern but you ↘ were!
↗ Who could ↘ blame me?" I tell the what's now a ↘ magnificent
↘ purple ↘ tetrahedron, eggplant-sized cilia straining at its corners, ↘
   just
a ↘ hint of ferniness remains in its fingertips—enough to ↘ blush.
We hug ↘ goodbye. The scent of ↘ flowers lingers around ↘ me
the next ↘ day. Flying ↗ home, a decorative airport fern that ↘ really
is a decorative airport fern ↘ says, "You smell ↘ nice." I ↘ don't
↘ believe it, but it's ↘ still a ↘ happy
↘ ending.

The end of the poem is particularly stunning—as the lines get shorter, the
falling pitches increase, and there's a growing sense of emphasis. Many
places where the hesitancy of a rising pitch would carry forward prose,
the falling pitch introduced by the line break slows the intonation and
adds heft, hitting the beats harder than they would in prose.

A Digression on the Recording of Poems

It is increasingly common for recordings of poems to be published alongside the text of the poem. The Limón and Knox poems were taken from
the *New Yorker* and Poets.org, respectively, but were both published
before these sources began providing recordings of poets reading their

own work. In a certain way, I did feel like I was cheating by not using poems with recordings that would allow me to check my work against the author's voice—but in a certain way, checking against their recorded voices would undermine the value that I am placing on print culture. I did not want the literal, human, recorded voices of Limón and Knox to be the arbiters of how the poem goes into the world as a printed poem—I wanted the poems to "speak" for themselves—to find the voice that the poem on the page conjures within the voice of a reader, though certainly I leave open the possibility of discovering that my own method of reading is not nearly as widespread as I am arguing that it is. And, of course, the *literal* speaker becomes me, rather than the author. This seems like an advantage to me, although I suspect in the future it will be seen as a form of readerly narcissism. It is also the case that once a voice is recorded, the intonations are fixed, and often in ways that are counterintuitive. I often think of the scene in *The Comeback*, where Lisa Kudrow's character tries to work out how to say her newly assigned catchphrase "I don't need to see that," shifting through every possibility of pitch, inflection, tone, and emphasis. Matt LeBlanc's unforgettable delivery of "How you doin'?" on *Friends* renders the language with a fixed interpretation. The pleasure is precisely in the specificity of the delivery that is *not* available on the page. I love *King Lear* so much that I can no longer watch the play, because I only see decisions that have been made by the actors and director, and I almost always think they've gotten the play wrong. Conversely, I love *Twelfth Night* so much that I see it over and over again because I love seeing the decisions made by the actors and director. It is a mystery to me why I love to see *Twelfth Night* reinterpreted, but can only enjoy *Lear* if it's the play I think it ought to be.

There may come a day when *not* having the audio file of a poet will be as strange to the readers of the future as having to use a knife to open the pages of a book is to us now—and when the word "reader" may be revised to "listener," "auditor," or some other nuanced descriptor. I tend not to use the phonetic transcriptions of words in the dictionary anymore, because using the *OED* online, I can simply press the "speaker" icon and hear the word spoken. It may be that poetry will become like popular music, so that recordings and covers are the main conduit for the distribution of poetry, but I suspect not. Print culture may merge with digital culture in ways that currently seem precious or sentimental, but that will preserve the aspect of writing going into the world to be read in the voice that the reader's brain provides.

Even when language is heard, there can still be inconsistencies. When I was in junior high school, my parents once spent weeks making fun of me for pronouncing "triumvirate" as "TRY-um-VIE-rate" (it's "try-UM-ver-ate") but I was just repeating what my teacher had said. I continue to insert the lost "rhotic r" into my favorite sci-fi villains, the Daleks, despite the fact that it's a backformation. "Dalek" has always been pronounced "Dah-lek," and as a British schoolchild in the very early 1980s, I too said "Dah-lek." But as my accent shifted from the expected forms of speech in Thetford, England to the expected forms of speech in Vacaville, California, I had to put "r"s back into most words that had the "ah" sound ("cahr" not "cah" and "park" not "pahk"). Naturally, I added one to "Dah-lek" and continue to say "Dar-lek" despite being corrected by friends and family. The relationship between written language and spoken language is complex. One advantage of written Chinese is that "the time-honored character-based writing system can readily accommodate different modes of pronunciation, even mutually unintelligible dialects" (Buruma, n. p.). Written English actually performs this feat more often than we give it credit for, but most of us only realize this fact when we need to turn on the subtitles for detective shows taking place in the most northern parts of Britain. One of the enduring facets of colonialism is that only marginalized people tend to have their language written in dialect—though dialect can be used to further marginalize speakers (as in the case of Margaret Mitchell) or to protectively retain linguistic difference (as in the case of Zora Neale Hurston).

If audio increases its presence to the point of superseding print, then my argument for the function of the written line will have no need to exist. If hearing largely replaces reading, then the interference will simply be present in the author's voice, and all this hand-wringing over the relationship between print and voice will seem beside the point. More likely, audio will not displace or replace text, in the same way that sheet music continues to be sold, but I will point out that sheet music may have more staying power than many audio recordings—in part because sheet music gives a talented musician more room to insert themselves. But I also find that recordings of poetry tend to date themselves faster than poems on the page. I quite like reading Plath's "Daddy" or Yeats's "Sailing to Byzantium," but I find the recordings of those poets reading those same poems to be uncomfortable at best, their voices as cringeworthy as 1980s greenscreen effects. On the other hand, listening to a recording of Gwendolyn Brooks reading "We Real Cool" was revelatory and changed the way I understood the poem—and may have been the moment when I began to form my understanding of the line as running interference with the intonation of the sentence.

A Digression on the Meanings of Writing Systems

While writing is a global phenomenon, what written language means (and has meant) varies from place to place. The heritage of the Greek alphabet, the Latin alphabet, and their colonial legacies is that those of us taught to write with alphabets see written language as a way to capture speech. However, writing that captures speech is not the only way to write. The Lakota Winter Count is a boustrophedonic history recorded in what we might call icons. Aristotle essentially regarded speech as clothing for thoughts that would otherwise be invisible, and writing as simply a record of speech. Derrida's foundational argument in his theory of deconstruction is "logocentrism," or the idea that Westerners have been lying to themselves, and that in fact, the written word is central—or comes first—rather than the spoken word. (Derrida later expands this concept to "phallologocentrism," insisting that masculine dominance is fundamental to written dominance.) But also central to deconstruction is the idea that language is not coherent—and that just as language becomes incoherent when insisting on the boundary between the terms of any binary, all language is designed for other purposes than the one seems to be attempting to achieve. Still, just as there are no atheists in foxholes, there are no deconstructionists calling 911. "Please send an ambulance; I am having trouble breathing" is a statement that suggests that language does sometimes have rather clear and direct meanings.

Other languages and cultures have different valences and values around the written word. Hebrew is referred to as "Loshen Kodesh," or "Holy Language," by some religious Jews, and there are Jewish sects that continue to use Yiddish as a day-to-day language in order to avoid using

Holy Language for quotidian purposes, even though Hebrew has been revived as a spoken language. In written Hebrew, letters have numerical values, vowels are not necessary for fluent speakers, and multiple words are built around three-letter roots that have consistent meanings. Much of the mysticism of the Kabbalah centers on performing a kind of textual analysis that would be impossible to apply to written English simply because the features of the language's orthography do not correspond neatly. The Torah is written entirely without punctuation marks, though there are codified arrangements of spacing, gaps, elongated letters, and decorative markings. While contemporary Hebrew has adopted Western punctuation marks, biblical Hebrew developed a set of punctuation marks that indicate to the reader/singer how to cantillate (or chant) the text; there's really nothing like this in English, even though those marks predated Western punctuation and are thought to have inspired the punctuation we currently use. A musician could reproduce the system with sheet music or something similar, but my larger point is that literacy is not precisely the same across all languages, and that the features of one's own language are most easily discerned in the context of other languages precisely because they differ so much.

Languages and writing systems are not symmetrical, and yet the technologies continue to echo each other. The Torah continues to be written on scrolls, resulting in a yearly "rewinding" of the scrolls in order to get back to the beginning. In the 1980s and 1990s, we had a similar experience, following the exhortation of the stickers on VHS tapes asking us to "be kind, rewind," but this after-viewing practice was superseded by DVDs and then streaming. The technology of spooled magnetic tape echoes the older technology of spooled parchment sheets. Because Old English was not written until after the invention of the codex (sheets bound to a spine), English texts have always been ones you can page through, rather than scroll through (and yet "scrolling" reasserts itself as one "scrolls" through digital texts). The codex was invented by Egyptian Christians (*Copts*) in the second century, and proved to be a stunningly convenient and lasting technology. Coptic binding was the first iteration of the codex, and remains widely practiced.

I hesitate to go much beyond the outlines of how other forms of writing work. Knowing that a language is tonal, or inflected, or holophrastic, or without gender, or without tense is interesting insofar as it indexes the ways that meaning can be made in ways dissimilar to English's techniques, but far too often serves to suggest impossibilities of communication or to suggest that some languages provide their speakers better or worse tools than other languages. Even in quoting experts, there is a kind of sentimentalism that often creeps in around the edges when discussing the linguistic features of forms of writing and language one has never studied or been immersed in. I also find a kind of credulity sneaks in. While it is true that writing has been done with knots—the knot writing of the Incans was said to contain all of Incan culture (Wolf, 48)—*The Irish Times* debunked a widely circulated urban-myth-turned-clickbait that Irish fisherman's sweaters were knit in such a way as to help identify the bodies of drowned sailors. They weren't (Boland, n. p.). In Paul Baker's study of Polari, in considering what exactly Polari *is* (a gay slang, a gay language, a gay argot?), he discusses the linguistic term "anti-language," to name "forms of language that are used by people who are somehow apart from mainstream society" (17). While I'm inclined to agree with Baker that "When you learned Polari, you weren't just learning the words but the attitude that went with them" (18), I'm not sure that this argument can be expanded past the specificities of any given anti-language.

Neuroscientist Maryanne Wolf explains that different parts of the brain are used to read different kinds of writing. Comparing the logographic demands of Chinese characters with the alphabetic demands of English letters, she writes, "When Chinese readers first try to read in English, their brains attempt to use Chinese-based neuronal pathways" (5), and vice versa. Over time, as the brain becomes fluent, the part of the brain that is used shifts. Brain imaging of people reading Japanese, which has both kanji (a logographic form of writing) and kana (an alphabetic form of writing), confirms that different parts of the brain are used for these different versions of writing (63). But without expertise, these facts are more interesting than useful, and every time I read the sentence, "The act of learning Chinese characters has literally shaped the Chinese reading brain" (5), I imagine an angry parent demanding that Chinese not be taught in their child's school so as not to rewire their child's brain.

The Sapir-Whorf hypothesis[12] is beyond the scope of this essay—though it may sound as though I am advocating a version of it. The Sapir-Whorf hypothesis posits that one's language determines how one thinks, often leading to ridiculous conclusions. However, I would agree with linguist Lera Boroditsky that language directs attention. When my parents were visiting me in Russia during my study abroad year in the 1990s, my host parents were telling my actual parents a story about a famous pilot who had died in a plane accident that he seemed too experienced to have caused. Russian has separate verbs for "to die of natural causes" and "to die of unnatural causes." I had only ever heard "to die of unnatural causes" used in cases where it would best be translated as "murder" or "kill." I was translating the story as one in which Stalin had murdered a rival—my host parents assured me that this was not the story they were telling. But it *was* the story they were implying.

Because I think a lot about sex and gender, I'm fascinated by how they work in languages. When I lived in Russia, I tried to introduce the phrase for "coming out of the closet" to my gay friends, but the closest I could get was something clumsy like "leaving the wardrobe" or "exiting the cabinet." In a recent article about Elliot Page in *Komsolmoskaya Pravda*, I discovered that Russians have adopted the notion of "coming out"—they call it «каминг аут», a direct transliteration (or phonetic transcription) of "coming out." In the late 90s, I found it quite odd that Russians tended to use imported words like "gay" (гей) and "boyfriend" (бойфренд) to describe themselves and their partners, rather than something homegrown—and yet I think that it only seemed strange to me because I'm used to those words and hear them as cognates. In Russian they provide clarity and spice, the same way I might choose to say "pied à terre" or "mise-en-scène" without feeling like English has failed me. Foreign borrowings often have a specificity or meaning in their new home that did not exist in their original language.

As more and more people resist binary gender, singular "they" has caught on in the US, while in Argentina the use of a gender-neutral "e" ending in place of "o" and "a" is widely used, doing much the same work that in the US had been done by the "x" in "Latinx" (Politi). I was greatly relieved by the introduction of "cis" as a prefix to "gender"—it seems more elegant to have "cisgender" at hand than the rather awkward "non-trans." All language is a thing in flux, and my experience is that we find the language for what we need to say, rather than having language limit what is thinkable. Foreign borrowings often provide narrower meanings which give the new word a tighter focus. The words "verse" and "poetry" have narrow meanings in English, but wider meanings in their language of origin.

My point in examining and contextualizing the history of written English is to show that the features of English language poetry's transcription are historically grounded rather than universal or natural, even though they share elements of many languages, and features of writing are often adopted by other languages (English literacy relies on Latin letters and Arabic numerals) when they prove useful. But continuing in this vein, where gender lives in language is far from consistent. In English, only our pronouns indicate gender. In Spanish, French, and German, the pronouns, adjectives, and nouns mark gender. In Russian, the pronouns, adjectives, nouns, and verbs (but only in the past tense) mark gender. The German word "Neuter"—to an English speaker at least—suggests the loss of gender, or rather the loss of male genitalia. (Pet owners might wonder why "spay" is not a gender.) But the corresponding grammatical Russian term is «средний род» or "middle gender," which suggests no loss. In writing about gendered pronouns, Deaf poet Meg Day writes, "Pronoun conversations continue to baffle and frustrate me. We don't have them in ASL; we have other problems, but not pronouns. I don't want to tell you what mine are. I don't want to put them in my email signature. I want you to call me by my name. No, not that one. With your hands" (n. p.).

My own experience of international influence is that while novels tend to travel fairly well between languages, music tends to have a sort of blurred edge that lets it slide between cultures, and visual arts tend to have a global immediacy, poetry doesn't quite have the same transferability across languages, or across cultures. In *Evgeny Onegin*, Pushkin's classic line "шла шла" (*shlah shlah*) is untranslatable—or rather the sense is translatable, but the sonic pleasure combined with the literal sense requires the line to be in Russian. "She walked walked" might capture the sense, but the power is lost. When Agha Shahid Ali brought the formal ghazal back into English, he was resisting the free-verse ghazal that had essentially been created and popularized by Adrienne Rich's translations of Ghalib in the 1960s. But the formal ghazal in many other countries is a sung form, and the pleasures of the spoken formal ghazal in English and the sung formal ghazal are not symmetrical. I think that this is Shklovsky's point when he says that art is passed from the uncle to the nephew. It's precisely the lack of symmetry that sparks creativity. In difference there is possibility.

Linefuck and the Persistence of Lineation

E. E. Cummings is generally considered the writer to have most engaged the material reality of typewritten manuscripts—but those experiments came long after the typewriter came into common use by a good sixty years. As long as typesetters were working from longhand manuscripts, things like the battle over how many spaces to leave after a period were moot arguments. I learned to leave two spaces to indicate a typed manuscript; published work would be copy edited and then typeset to follow the rules of typesetting.

Over the course of the twentieth century, the process of first draft, to typist, to edited draft, to copy editor, to typesetter, to publisher became codified, and then disintegrated. I was the first generation of college students to have WYSIWYG (What you see is what you get) word processing programs. In high school, I typed my papers in a version of the program Enable that allowed me to do exciting things like italicize, footnote, and insert fractions, but I could not see them on the screen—I had to print to be sure that my formatting was actually in place. At the University of Maryland in the 1990s, there were professors who insisted on maintaining the distinction between manuscript and publication— for example, they expected us to use underlining in manuscript; italics were for publication. In the year 2001, when I was Phillis Levin's assistant on *The Penguin Book of the Sonnet*, we received page galleys that we copy edited and returned with proofreader's marks. When I edited *Queer: A Reader for Writers* for Oxford University Press in 2016, the galley pages were edited with an ad hoc version of PDF notations. I did not miss the hefty manuscripts and the postmark deadlines, but working in an ad hoc system reintroduced a great deal of ambiguity that the proofreader's marks had elegantly eliminated. My experience in 2016 was much simpler in some ways, but it lacked the elegance and clarity of my experience in 2001.

I'm borrowing the term "linefuck" from the queer 1990s term

"genderfuck"[13]—which indicates that one is not done with gender, but that there is both pleasure and productive thought in breaking the rules while playing the game. What I'm calling linefuck is not simply the use of imagery. What I'm calling linefuck is a refusal of the line as a repeatable unit of sound. Linefuck is linefuck because the line is there—you can see lines—yet these lines will not yield to any kind of analysis that's been presented up until this point. The concept (gender, the line) persists, but the familiar is bent in ways that make it unfamiliar or uncanny; the newness is not precisely that there is a new system in place—as when one goes from the Anglo-Saxon line with its steady beats, midline caesuras, and alliterations to the metric patterns of Middle English poetry—but rather that the system is in place in unrecognizable ways.

Consider Leila Chatti's "Zina." In this poem, she uses numbers to rearrange the way in which the line is read. These are the opening five lines:

① *Verily, it was heaven.*

③ *allow me* ② *I couldn't be certain You would*

⑤ *so I sought my own* ④ *admission*

⑥ *in the body*

⑦ *of a man.*

(1–5)

The poem is right-justified, and the way to read is self-evident to anyone who has ever done a connect-the-dots picture, and yet how this impacts the reading of the poem is unclear. For example, in "③allow me ②I couldn't be certain You would," what is the nature of the break as the reader completes clause 2, and then returns, not to the next line, but to the same line? The break is almost the same—the eye reaching the right margin before returning to the left—but here, after the return to the left margin, the reading stops, and then slips to the next line, in the middle.

Marwa Helal makes a similar revision to the line in her poem "Who Real" but whereas Chatti moves clauses and phrases out of order, Helal reverses the line completely, reordering each word from right to left. In this small excerpt from the poem, she's questioned about the effect:

asks poem this of draft shorter a see to professor first the
device stylistic this sustain could i long how

think you do long how 'prof dunno i 'w counter i
™ pneumoic hegemonic demonic heteronormative khwhite the
itself sustain can
rage road and clown class the all and american im now
be never could i

(25–31)

Helal explicitly connects the conventions of standard written English to
systemic racism, and in reversing the order of the words (but not flipping
the poem itself, and putting a mirror image to the reader), Helal forces
the reader to find a new way through the line. Standard written English
is resisted in other aspects, like the exclusive use of lowercase letters and
the sonic "kh" prefixing "white" to alter its pronunciation, though I think
linefuck makes the greatest demand on the reader. The eye goes from left
to right to read each word, but then has to move left after each word to
get to the next word. The poem resists the line, while it relies on the line.
The line is attacked and entrenched at the same time.

Coda

I don't think that we are at the end of the (poetic) line, even though shifts
in the structure of writing have made it possible for us to examine the
line in a new way. I've considered three major technological shifts that
have changed the poetic line: the shift from an oral to literary culture, the
shift from manuscript to moveable type, the invention of the typewriter,
and the invention of WYSIWYG word processing and the internet. In
each case, the previous version of poetry was not superseded, but rather
revised. As much as black-and-white films continue to be made by choice
rather than necessity, print culture will persist, even as digital modes of
production, reproduction, and distribution become the norm. I hope
that what has not gotten lost here is that I *love* the poetic line, and I am
fiercely protective of the line, even as I see it shifting in the digital winds
that are blowing across the face of the literary earth.

The line is a source of endless conversation among poets: what it is,
how it works, how it should work, how it does work. In undertaking this
essay, I wanted to see if I could understand the line both as an essential
grounding principle for poetry and as a historically dynamic conceptual-

ization. In borrowing a notation from English language textbooks, I hope I was able to make visible the way that I see the line working, and how I understand the basics of sentence intonation that the line runs interference against. I hope that my particular contribution to an understanding of how the line works in English will be adopted by other poets and scholars, even though I know that it requires a new notation that has not been used in poetry, despite having been discussed in terms that are not quite the ones I have used.

I came to poetry because it was the only place I felt honest. As a younger person, the sentence in prose felt fundamentally dishonest to me, or rather, my own sentences in prose felt like lies. I was so aware of what I was not saying or excluding in each of my declarative sentences that the act of writing prose slightly sickened me. In part, I pursued a PhD after my MFA in poetry because I had developed an intense fear of writing prose. Poetry let me have a sense that I could calibrate the sentence through the line break and that I could find a way to tell the truth by signaling the reader what it was that lay just outside the declarative. I've come to feel at home in the essay, in part because I learned to embrace the digression and to inhabit the paragraph as a unit of communication. My gratitude toward the line as a structure has been implicit in my work as a poet, but I hope that in this essay, I can honor the line as a structure that has nurtured and carried me forward as a thinker and a person. When I felt most alone, it was poems that kept me company.

Acknowledgments

My deepest gratitude to poet and medievalist Professor Katharine Jager for her help in shaping my understanding of medieval writing and literature. Any errors are my own.

The composition of this essay was supported by a grant from the Professional Staff Congress of the City University of New York.

Notes

1. The distinction between "doggerel" and "light verse" is a bit like the distinction between "pornography" and "erotica"—meaningful, but subjective, and with significant overlap.

2. Deconstruction asserts itself here again: Derrida uses the term "logocentrism" to name the primacy of writing over speaking in Western thought (opposing Aristotle's notion that speaking makes thought visible and that writing makes speech visible).

3. When two people buy a house, they can be "tenants in common" and each own 50 percent of the house, or "tenants in joint" who both own 100 percent of the house. Poetry is the latter for me—the written word and the spoken voice both own 100 percent of the poem.

4. At the beginning of *The Bluest Eye*, Toni Morrison reprints a passage from a Dick and Jane book three times. The first time, the passage is punctuated fully. In the second version, the punctuation has been removed; the text is entirely lowercase (save the initial letter), but spaces remain between words. In the final version, all spaces between words, all punctuation, and all capital letters (again, save the initial "H") have been removed. This final version is *scriptio continua*, but has the effect of overwhelming the contemporary reader because what is needed to make meaning is gone. To punctuate that passage would have been the subject of many an ancient education.

5. According to Powell, literacy creates words and their boundaries. Speakers of purely oral languages do not have the same concept of discrete words and word boundaries that we learn along with reading.

6. The version I am using here takes the orthography from the Digital Index of Medieval Verse, but the punctuation comes from Parkes.

7. Thank you to Katharine Jager for her help with my understanding of this poem.

8. For a very full discussion of the sounds the letter yogh made, see John Frankis's "Layamon and the Fortunes of Yogh," in which he considers how best to render "Laȝamon," which has been variously written as Layamon, Lawman, Lazamon, Lagamon, and Lawomon, among other spellings.

9. My understanding of slurs is that they are used to dehumanize an "other" and make it acceptable for someone to do violence to the members of the group being slurred—in other words, they make the other into an object. However, when the slur boomerangs back, and the speaking voice adopts the slur as a subject, the dehumanizing quality is challenged because the speaking voice asserts the humanity of the speaker. I don't wish to be seen as saying that the word "fag" was not a slur in the 1960s, or that it wasn't a signifier of violence; I do want to say that archival use of the slur requires a more complex response than simply condemnation or acceptance—and that the reproduction of the slur intact is key to maintaining an accurate archival record.

10. For readers interested in learning to scan and hear meter and rhythm in poetry, I have found no better guide than Alfred Corn's *The Poem's Heartbeat*. For a critique of centering sound in poetry as an ableist reading practice, I would refer the reader to Meg Day's essay "Sound Consequence."

11. My understanding of Grossman's conception has been deeply influ-

enced by Tom Sleigh's lectures on the topic of the line, which he delivered at NYU when I was his student in 1999. These lectures are unpublished.

12. For an excellent and accessible discussion of the history and implications of the Sapir-Whorf hypothesis, see Basel Al-Sheikh Hussein, "The Sapir-Whorf Hypothesis Today," *Theory & Practice in Language Studies (TPLS)* 2, no. 3 (March 2012): 642–46.

13. For a fuller discussion of "genderfuck," see June Reich's "Genderfuck: The Law of the Dildo," listed in the works cited.

Works Cited

Auden, W. H. *Collected Poems*, ed. Edward Mendelson. Knopf, 1991.

Baker, Paul. *Fabulosa! The Story of Polari, Britains Secret Gay Language*. Reaktion Books, 2019.

Baraka, Amiri. *SOS: Poems 1961–2013*, selected by Paul Vandelisti. Grove, 2014.

Boland, Rosita. "Aran Jumper Myths Debunked." *The Irish Times*, March 17, 2018.

Boroditsky, Lara. "How the Languages We Speak Shape the Ways We Think." *The Cambridge Handbook of Psycholinguistics*, ed. Michael Spivey, et al. Cambridge University Press, 2012. ProQuest Ebook Central.

briansully. "Valerie Cherish." YouTube, March 14, 2014, https://www.youtube .com/watch?v=7zvU2E9s4us

Bright, James Wilson. *Bright's Old English Grammar & Reader*, 3rd ed. Ed. by Frederic G. Cassidy and Richard N. Ringler. Holt, 1971.

Britannica Academic, Encyclopedia Britannica, s.v., "Antistrophe," accessed January 12, 2022. academic-eb-com.bmcc.ezproxy.cuny.edu/levels/collegi ate/article/antistrophe/124777

Buruma, Ian. "How the Chinese Language Got Modernized." *The New Yorker*, January 17, 2022.

Butterfield, Ardis. "Why Medieval Lyric?" *ELH*, 82, no. 2 (2015): 319–43. https://doi.org/10.1353/elh.2015.0017

Carson, Anne. *Eros the Bittersweet*. Dalkey Archive Press, 1986.

Chatti, Leila. *Deluge*. Copper Canyon, 2020.

Day, Meg. "Sound Consequence." *Poetry Foundation*. November 30, 2021.

Dickinson, Emily. *The Poems of Emily Dickinson*, ed. R. W. Franklin. The Belknap Press of Harvard University Press, 1999.

Digital Index of Middle English Verse, s.v., "Trusty seldom . . ." https://www.di mev.net/record.php?recID=6077#wit-6077-1

Finch, Annie. *The Ghost of Meter: Culture and Prosody in American Free Verse*. University of Michigan Press, 1993.

Findell, Martin. *Runes*. The British Museum, 2014.

Frankis, John. "Layamon and the Fortunes of Yogh." *Medium Aevum* 73, no. 1 (June 2004): 1–9. EBSCOhost. https://search-ebscohost-com.bmcc.ezproxy.cuny.edu/login.aspx?direct=true&db=lfh&AN=13870155&site=ehost-live&scope=site

Fukuyama, Francis, *The End of History and the Last Man*. The Free Press, 2006.

Grossman, Allen and Mark Halliday. *The Sighted Singer: Two Works on Poetry for Readers and Writers*. Johns Hopkins University Press, 1992.

Hart, Ellen Louise and Martha Nell Smith. *Open Me Carefully: Emily Dickinson's Intimate Letters to Susan Huntington Dickinson*, 1st ed. Paris Press, 1998.

Helal, Marwa. "Who Real." Academy of American Poets Poem-a-Day, August 27, 2020. https://poets.org/poem/who-real

"Intonation in English Pronuciation." Learn English Today. https://www.learn-english-today.com/pronunciation-stress/intonation.html

Jager, Katharine. "'A Clateryng of Knokkes': Multimodality and Performativity in 'The Blacksmith's Lament.'" Sounding Out, May 2, 2016. https://soundstudiesblog.com/2016/05/02/a-clateryng-of-knokkes-multimodality-and-performativity-in-the-blacksmiths-lament/

Kierkegaard, Søren. "On Himself." *Existentialism from Dostoevsky to Sartre*, ed. Walter Kaufmann. Pickle Partners Publishing, 2016.

Knox, Jennifer L. "The Decorative Airport Fern Is Not What It Pretends to Be." Academy of American Poets, 2011. https://poets.org/poem/decorative-airport-fern-not-what-it-pretends-be

Limón, Ada. "State Bird." *The New Yorker*, May 26, 2014. https://www.newyorker.com/magazine/2014/06/02/state-bird

The New Princeton Encyclopedia of Poetry and Poetics. Ed. Alex Preminger et al. Princeton University Press, 1993. s.v. "Strophe."

The New Princeton Encyclopedia of Poetry and Poetics. Ed. Alex Preminger et al. Princeton University Press, 1993. s.v. "Verse."

OED Online, Oxford University Press, s.v., "poetry, n.," accessed January 12, 2022. www.oed.com/view/Entry/146552

OED Online, Oxford University Press, s.v., "verse, n.," accessed January 12, 2022. www.oed.com/view/Entry/222685

Parkes, M. B. *Pause and Effect: An Introduction to the History of Punctuation in the West*. University of California Press, 1993.

Politi, Daniel. "In Argentina, a Bid to Make Language Gender Neutral Gains Traction." *New York Times*, April 15, 2020.

Powell, Barry B. *Writing: Theory and History of the Technology of Civilization*. Wiley-Blackwell, 2009.

Reed, John. "Lost Generation." YouTube, November 30, 2007. https://www.youtube.com/watch?v=42E2fAWM6rA

Reich, June L. "Genderfuck: The Law of the Dildo." *Discourse* 15, no. 1 (1992): 112–27. http://www.jstor.org/stable/41389251

Schmandt-Besserat, Denise. *How Writing Came About*. University of Texas Press, 1996.

Shklovsky, Victor. *Viktor Shklovsky: A Reader*, ed. Alexandra Berlina. Bloomsbury Academic, 2016.

Sondheim, Stephen. "You Could Drive a Person Crazy." *Company: Original Broadway Cast*, 1970. Spotify.

Still Watching Netflix. "Every Time Joey Says How You Doin'? In Friends | Netflix." YouTube, March 30, 2021. https://www.youtube.com/watch?v=X1qTyZI_VlM

Vadde, Aarthi. "Platform or Publisher." *PMLA: Publications of the Modern Language Association of America*, 136, no. 3 (May 2021): 455–62.

Van Gelderen, Elly. *A History of the English Language*. John Benjamins Publishing Company, 2014.

Wolf, Maryanne. *Proust and the Squid: The Story and Science of the Reading Brain*. Harper Perennial, 2008.

How the Sonnet Turns

From a Fold to a Helix

In Phillis Levin's introduction to *The Penguin Book of the Sonnet*, she writes that "fourteen lines do not guarantee a sonnet: it is the behavior of those lines in relation to each other—their choreography—that identifies the form" (xxxvii–xxxviii). Later she explains, "We could say that for the sonnet, the *volta* is the seat of its soul" (xxxix). The volta, or the turn, is crucial to the identity of the sonnet. For many theorists, the volta itself marks not merely the emergence of a new form, but the formal embodiment of early modern subjectivity.[1] As Paul Oppenheimer puts it, quite bluntly, "Modern thought and literature began with the invention of the sonnet" (3). Oppenheimer stresses that the sonnet is the first poetic form meant to be read silently—and that silent reading was still something of a novelty. Medieval poetry focused heavily on allegory, externalizing conflicts with the goal of finding spiritual unity with a distant god (9). The sonnet placed conflict at the personal level, treating the divided self *as* a divided self (24). Oppenheimer celebrates the sonnet for introducing a structure that was at once mathematical, logical, and personal. "If an emotional problem were to be resolved in a mere fourteen lines, and in isolation, it would have to be resolved in a particular way: by the poet and the poet themselves, and within the mind of the poet. There was no one else, no outside, no audience. It was in perceiving this, and then creating a poetry to match, that Giacomo [inventor of the sonnet] arrived at a stroke of genius that was to lead to major changes in how most poets and other writers were to write ever since" (24). In other words, the volta indexes an interiority that is indicative of how we understand ourselves and our art. The turn is necessarily a turn inwards, a divided self that need not distribute its warring factions across a series of allegorical selves, but rather presents a self that is defined by its own contradictions.

Levin begins her sonnet anthology with a proem, a Chaucer translation of Petrarch's 132 into his own "Canticus Troili," or "The Song of Troilus" from his "Troilus and Criseyde." The poem begins "If no love is, O God, what fele I so?" (1) and ends "For hete of cold, for cold of heat, I dye" (21). This is crucial, because it marks the paradox of the divided self—that one might freeze *and* burn, that one might deny love's existence while also suffering from love's existence. In rather broad terms, taking over from the unitary self of medieval Christendom. I often explain this shift in "subjectivity" to my students by comparing *Everyman*, the medieval miracle play from the 1400s, to *Hamlet*. The title character of *Everyman* wants simply to have fun and not to die. But when the character Death comes for Everyman, Everyman goes to the afterlife, as he must, only with the character Good-Deeds in tow, leaving behind Fellowship, Goods, and Beauty—characters in the play. Internal desires blend with externalized objects of desire, cast as characters in a play and distributed among actors. The title character of *Hamlet*, on the other hand, is a bit of mystery to himself, and spends a great deal of time figuring out what he thinks, and often inquires into how, as one person, he might decide among the options that are offered by the various facets of his own divided self. Hamlet's divisions are internal—and while King Hamlet's ghost can be read as a holdover from that medieval impulse to externalize aspects of the self—Hamlet is one person with many desires, but a single life to act in (or not act in). We sometimes read the divided self back onto texts where it is unwarranted. For a contemporary audience, it makes sense to read the witches in *Macbeth* as an aspect of Macbeth's divided self, but Shakespeare's audiences really did believe in witches, and King James wrote a whole book on how to spot them. Chaucer's Troilus encounters love as a proto-form of division—as a paradox; he doesn't have quite the labyrinthine psyche of Hamlet, but that's about two hundred years or so in the future, waiting to arrive in English and England alongside the European sonnet.[2] The sonnet in English first found purchase in translations like Chaucer's, then through translations by Sir Thomas Wyatt that retained the fourteen-lined sonnet form we know as the Italian or Petrarchan sonnet, and then Henry Howard, Earl of Surrey, innovated the form by moving the volta to between the twelfth line and the final couplet, originating what we now know as the Shakespearian or English Sonnet (Levin, lii–liii). Still, the way we use "sonnet" is a slightly later addition—originally in English, "sonnets," from the Italian "sonneti" or "little sound" (Oppenheimer, 173), indicating any poem meant to be read by the spoken voice or even silently, rather than sung as lyrics to a melody. Silent reading was a novel development of the early modern period (24).

If you accept this argument, that the defining quality of the sonnet is this embodiment of the divided self that defines modern subjectivity, then the power of the division is that it captures not only the way we understand ourselves, but the way we think and the way we experience the world and ourselves in the world. I have argued before that received poetic forms demand a rhetorical mode. Most obviously, the ghazal, which is much older than the sonnet, makes an unusual demand on the Western writer in demanding that the writer avoid the unities of narrative, argument, persona, or monologue, and requires a multifaceted meditation on a topic, approaching a single concern, captured in the refrain, and returned to from multiple angles. That is to say, you can't rewrite your sonnet as a ghazal (or your ghazal as a sonnet) because the ghazal's structural demands are also rhetorical demands. The sestina and the villanelle demand an obsessive approach, because nothing short of obsession will allow the writer to return so constantly to the repeated parts of the poem. J. V. Cunningham, in his defense of poetic form, wrote, "it is apparent to any poet who sets out to write a sonnet that the form of the sonnet is the content, and its content the form. This is not a profundity, but the end of the discussion" (222). I, however, will reopen the discussion, in part because my initial intention for this essay was simply to elaborate the ways that the volta might form the sonnet, and I find myself instead making an argument about the additional possibilities of the sonnet— possibilities I was quite surprised to discover as I sat down to study some of my favorite sonnets. My initial purpose in exploring the sonnet's turn was simply to look at the ways in which different sonnets had approached the necessary turn. I had intended to consider what might be connected on either side of the hinging volta: an octave of a riddle that is solved in the sestet; a problem posed in the octave that finds an answer in the sestet; a confusion explored in the octave that is synthesized in the sestet; a change in speaker from octave to sestet; a situation laid out in the octave that is commented upon or given meaning in the sestet, and so on and so on. And you can certainly substitute douzaine and couplet for octave and sestet in these paradigms, though typically the Shakespearean sonnet has a small shift after the octave, and then a hard turn going into the couplet. I had hoped to make an argument that the volta is a bit like a line break—that it happens in the space between one thing and another—and that if I could think about the volta as being like a line break, it might be a space to analyze lyric leaps and the lyric landings: that Ovidian metamorphic moment where one thing becomes another thing. That may still be true. And had I been determined to discover only what I had intended to find, I could have ignored the sonnets that did not fit my argument and move on. However, when I began to consider the poems that I had expected to be able to analyze in terms of the volta, I found that I was often not able to support my own argument, and that the single hinge I had been looking for was, well, not the main action. I was discovering poems that were more sinuous in their structure, and I settled on the figure of a helix as a way of describing the rhetorical motion of these sonnets.

Shortly, I will make my case by looking at sonnets that spiral, but first I would like to look at a sonnet that I think hinges nicely, just so that we can have a sense of what the expected motion of a sonnet is, how I would describe it, and what we are not talking about. Consider Julia Alvarez's untitled poem from her sonnet sequence 33.

Let's make a modern primer for our kids:
A is for Auschwitz; B for Biafra;
Chile; Dachau; El Salvador; F is
the Falklands; Grenada; Hiroshima
stands for H; Northern Ireland for I;
J is for Jonestown; K for Korea;
L for massacres in Lidice; My Lai;
N, Nicaragua; O, Okinawa;
P is the Persian Gulf and Qatar, Q;
Rwanda; Sarajevo—this year's hell;
T is for Treblinka and Uganda U;
Vietnam and Wounded Knee. What's left to spell?
An X to name the countless disappeared
when they are dust in Yemen or Zaire.

(72)

We should note that this particular poem is running a double structural feat—it is both an abecedarian and a sonnet. The abecedarian always limits a poem—or rather it reveals the limits of the poem's length to the reader. Once you see how long each letter will be allotted, the duration of the poem is preordained. This is also true of all fixed forms, like the sonnet, villanelle, or sestina; however, the abecedarian has a kind of accordion stretch to it, Merrill's almost book-length abecedarian, "The Book of Ephraim," being the longest I know, and Robert Pinsky's truly minimalist poem "ABC," which is only twenty-six words long (twenty-seven if you count the equal sign), being the shortest. The abecedarian is frequently a list poem, requiring knowledge of a particular topic (my own abecedarian was about film directors because I knew I could get from Almodóvar to Zefferelli). I always like to point out that the abecedarian is a common form of Hebrew prayer, which at least in Jewish lore is designed to prevent worshippers from becoming lost in prayer—the alphabet limits the amount of time one can spend in praise. The crucial thing is that the abecedarian, as a list poem, is both expansive in suggesting that one could go on forever and contractive in requiring the limitation of the listing to twenty-six letters as guide ropes that bring the reader along a prescribed course. In Alvarez's poem, the abecedarian plays the same dual role of limitation and expansion, but with the opposite impulse to prayer—we are drawn into atrocity rather than devotion. A Hebrew farmer must put down the prayer book by the *tav* (the last letter in the Hebrew alphabet) and get back to his fields, tempting as it may be to fall into worship. You, contemporary reader of English language poetry, must leave Alvarez's poem by Z, tempting as it might be to fall into the pit of despair opened by this historical list. And yet, with the artificial limitation of the abecedarian, one knows that the litany continues. And we do find a hinge between the abecedarian and the sonnet form at the letter "X." The X does double duty. In any abecedarian, the X is always the hardest letter to pull off because so few words begin with X. Alvarez uses it as a placeholder, the algebraic X that must be solved for, as well as the mapmaker's X, the X that marks the proverbial spot. And X, shouldering a massive burden in the poem, marks the beginning of the couplet, so the turn or volta is being marked as the lyric landing from the douzaine's leap.

A Shakespearean or English sonnet nonpareil, this poem is divided into a clear douzaine and couplet. The opening line establishes the abece-darian of atrocity, and then for twenty-six letters, essentially covers the same territory. Sonic repetition has the twin powers of emphasis and absurdity, but here, the repetition is structural rather than sonic, and the reader is brought deeper and deeper into the sense of horror, each letter an easily ticked-off terror, the hinge just before the final couplet at, "What's left to spell?" opening up onto those lost to history. In other words, the douzaine catalogs known atrocity,[3] and the couplet refracts that exhausting catalog of the known by reminding us that what we know is merely the tip of the iceberg, and that the unknown atrocities of human history far outnumber the known. Brilliantly, in using X to mark the "countless disappeared," Alvarez returns the reader to the individual humans who have suffered. "Auschwitz" and "Wounded Knee" are place-holders for enormous populations of murdered and betrayed people. We need the geographical name to remind us, and yet the true enormity of suffering, evoked in the couplet, reminds us of both the necessity and the inadequacy of how history is recorded. The douzaine marks the places we associate with atrocity, while the couplet refers us back to the people, letting the two forms of memory and history reverberate against each other. If I had begun with this sonnet, I might have been able to make my originally intended argument. The douzaine establishes the vastness of human suffering, as exhaustive as the places on Earth. The couplet comments on this mapped vastness by showing that this list is not even remotely exhaustive, but ongoing, and however bad it seemed, it is even worse.

Now, let us consider another poem from earlier in that same sequence.

Mami asks what I'm up to, and that means men
in any declension except sex; it
means do I realize I am thirty-
three without a husband, house, or children
and going on thirty-four? Papi extends
an invitation to come live with them,
there are two empty bedrooms I can write
in and handouts until I make it big
which means men at publication parties
asking me what mentors shaped my style

and has anyone told me how beautiful
I am having written something worthwhile?
Their drinks tinkle in their hands like keys
to doors closed at the closing of stories

(59)

Does this fold? Is there a turn? I can force one. I can say that the couplet marks a distinct change in sound and sense, and that Alvarez uses
the power of image in the final two lines to release the reader from the
hold of the power of argument and narration in the douzaine. I can say
a lot about the chiastic structure of the couplet—the density of conso-
nance, assonance, and pacing in the final lines suggests a distinct change
in soundwork from the conversational leisure of the preceding twelve
lines. I can point out the way the three short "i" sounds in "drinks,"
"tinkle," and "in" precede a series of long vowel sounds in "like," "keys,"
"doors," "closed," "closing," and "stories." The five "k"s across the two lines
("drinks," "tinkle," "keys," "closed," "closing") and the seven "s"s ("drinks,"
"keys," "doors," "closed," "closing," "stories") mark a kind of intoxicating
sonic density. The soundwork in that final couplet would make Gerard
Manley Hopkins blush, but is it a turn? I think it's not, precisely, or not
in the way that is typically meant. Rather, the poem spins out from the
very beginning, turning back on the question of fertility and isolation. In
this poem, I see a kind of tumble, a kind of helix. Unlike the abecedarian
sonnet, this opens with a story that we tumble through, the way her parents can only see literary success *as* success if it results in a man. The couplet does not steer to a resolution of a crisis, present another perspective,
answer her parents' impositions, or reflect her own ambivalence. Rather,
the poem begins with her parents imposing a somewhat severe vision of
how the public and literary might work with the private and domestic.
They want her public success as an author to lead to domestic success
(on their terms) as a wife, and presumably mother. Her parents are on
board with the speaker's goals for her own life on the precondition that
they can subordinate her goals to their own. Fame and publication are all
well and good, if they lead to a better class of husband. Like the old jokes
about women who have to attend graduate school because they failed to
get their MRS degree as undergraduates, her parents see literary ambition
as giving her access to a better class of marriageable material, discounting

the very goals they seem to be encouraging as they offer material support.

Alvarez's poem opens by exposing this odd private/public double bind. Her mother opens a conversation about men as a conversation about marriage, or rather as about anything but sex. The private and public are clearly bounded, and intimately but unspeakably linked. Her father joins in to offer a kind of support that can lead to meeting men who will find her work alluring. The poem keeps folding over the unsayable sexuality, the slight shame of needing material support, the goals of literary ambition, and the marketing of Alvarez's prospective literary success as a form of aphrodisiac. The poem spirals out from the speaker's discomfort at having her literary ambition pimped out by her parents, an unspoken and unspeakable version of sex that is everywhere for being nowhere, and can be neither dispelled nor embraced. The spiral continues as the concerns of the poem tumble forth, offers of support needed, goals shared, but not shared. The final couplet arrives as the encapsulation of all these strands: a literary party that may or may not lead to sex, that may or may not lead to romance, that may or may not lead to marriage. The awkward mingle, in which her parents show up in their desire for her to marry, for her to find a man, to find support, is also a fearful ending. The door that closes, the keys that lock—the domestic is both a refuge and a trap, especially for women married to men. The moment of arrival, of publication and celebration, also threatens to be the moment of enclosure and isolation. The poem spirals through these concerns, rather than folds or hinges. The couplet makes no advance in the sense of argument, but rather embodies the strands of contradiction, anxiety, desire, and silence. The first poem quite clearly turns at the volta, but the second poem spins out like a helix, doubling over itself in a whirl that the final lines encapsulate rather than reverse.

I'd like to turn now to William Meredith's, "The Illiterate." The poem begins, "Touching your goodness" (1), and then moves into an extended simile, comparing the experience of touching to "you" to being "like a man" (1) with a letter he cannot read. The first eight lines of the poem set up the position of the man, and the final six lines contemplate what the letter might say before opening the final couplet with, "What would you call his feeling" (13), ending on the complex unknowability of love. This poem uses the initial structure of Giacomo da Lentino's sonnets, which is the use of repeated end-words in place of rhymes. Meredith's homophones as end-words would be enough for its own essay, and I will make a little argument about why they're sexy—but they will not be our major focus, though they do manage to pull focus in a way that is part of my argument. The poem begins with an extended simile, comparing the touch of the addressed to the experience of having a letter that cannot be read by the recipient. The octave introduces the simile, and conjures the illiterate man holding the first letter he has ever been sent. The sestet considered three possibilities of what the letter might say, and in the final couplet, the poem asks the reader how they might name the emotions of the illiterate protagonist called into being to illuminate the impossibility of describing the touch from the first line.

The poem, on first reading, divides quite easily into the octave and the sestet—the rhyme scheme, or rather the repeated end-words, suggest the Italianate sonnet, creating an expectation that the volta will come in the shift between line 8 and line 9, and indeed the poem does have a stanza break, and it does shift. The octave sets up an extended simile about an illiterate man's experience of a letter being like the experience of touching the addressee of the poem. The sestet then offers up possibilities of what the letter might hold, and then asks the reader to reflect on what that experience of indeterminate not-knowing (which recreates the New Critical scene of indeterminacy) might be like. If we look for the trace of the Shakespearean, we do find that the poem turns yet again—that the final couplet, though allied with the possibilities offered in the sestet, actually turns back to the reader, and away from the simile itself—or rather reiterates the possibilities of the sestet succinctly while turning back to the reader.

And yet this neat division, of 8 and 6, or perhaps 8, 4, and 2, feels overdetermined to me. Finding the volta—at least in this poem—becomes a kind of confirmation bias, and the structural elements distract us from the other ways that the poem moves. I'm not suggesting that the turn and the volta are not present in the expected places, but rather that these sonnet-y markers mask something else that is going on in the poem. I want to turn to those other things that might be turning, in order to reconsider the motion from a single fold, or perhaps a double fold (a trifold?), into what I'm suggesting begins to look more like a helix or spiral.

The poem is built on repeating end-words rather than rhymes. The repeated words, except for "man" and "him" and "beloved," are homophones—"hand" meaning handwriting as well as a literal hand, "means" meaning both the sense of something as well as the way to do something, and "word" meaning a message as well as the actual units of speech. "One" is a relative pronoun, but revised from "anyone" to "someone." However, three end-words remain stable in their meaning: "him," "beloved," and "man." In 1958, for Meredith to have come out as a gay man would have been impossible. Indeed, in 1958 the metaphor of "coming out" still referred to debutantes, not the "closet," which is a post-Stonewall metaphor that bent the old phrase of "coming out" to a new sense. I've made the argument elsewhere that form can act as a kind of closet, or a kind of one-way mirror, directing one audience toward one meaning and another audience toward another,[4] but here the central- ity of these terms creates a stability and solidity to the love poem. The beloved gets lost in the simile as it plays out over the poem, and only the spine of "him," "beloved," and "man" anchors us to the desire and devo- tion that Meredith evokes in the poem. I generally have little patience with arguments for reading pre-Stonewall work by gay authors as need- ing queer decoder rings—especially in the case of John Ashbery—but in this case, I don't think I'm projecting as much as I am bringing forward aspects of the poem that reveal, rather than obscure.

Let's trace the "you" in the poem. We use "you" in roughly three ways in English poetry—as a general case ("How do you get to the train sta- tion?" "How do you know if you have measles?"), as an overheard direct address ("You do not do / You do not do"), or as a direct address to the reader ("What you have heard is true").[5] In this poem, we slip almost imperceptibly from an overheard direct address to a beloved into a direct address to the reader. As the poem spins forward, the beloved falls away, linguistically replaced by the reader in the final line. In the first line, the "you" is a beloved. "Touching your goodness, I am like a man" (1) sets off the poem, and we have the sense of overhearing. As the reader, we witness the speaker address his beloved, creating a simile to explain his feeling at the touch of the you. "You" returns in the thirteenth line as the reader. "What would you call his feeling" (13) is a direct address to the reader, who has followed the simile for twelve lines, finally arriving at this little quiz. How did the "you" slip from the beloved to the reader? How did the dyad of the ich/du lovers in line one become a triangle, with the dyad becoming reader/writer? In this motion, the beloved, seen one way, disappears—and in another way becomes an object rather than a subject. If you read queerly, it's a brilliant innovation. The reader is implicated in queer desire, by finding the subject of queer love both unnamable and beautiful, the vortex arriving not at resolution, but at the failure of language in the face of desire. And if you want a little gender nonconformity in your pre-Stonewall hangover from inversion, note that the first line says "I am like a man," if you go for the line break as being a preserver of meaning.

While this poem at first seems to hinge neatly between octave and sestet, I would argue that it actually spirals out across the unknowability—or unspeakability—of love. The octave moves into an extended simile about having a text that cannot be read without help, and the sestet puts forth possibilities for the text's meaning, and yet the frame of the simile almost disappears despite being the heart of the poem. The touch of the you and the desire of the beloved hover beside, inside, and beneath the simile, emerging only at the beginning and the end. The hinge hides the way the poem is a queer helix spiraling down as it enfolds its subject. In this case, the helix both contains and reveals the beloved—and while I have another obsession with the ways that both elegies and love poems exist on a continuum between those that center the lover and those that center the beloved, there's something that I find compelling about the poem folding around the beloved, to both encase and reveal him, like clever lighting for a nude scene in a play.

I want to jump forward in time to Terrance Hayes. His 2018 collection *American Sonnets for My Past and Future Assassin* is a collection of sonnets, each sonnet bearing the same title as the collection. The poems in the book are extremely varied, and have a kind of intimacy that touches one at the core in surprising ways. The sonnet that I'll consider, beginning "The umpteenth thump on the rump of a badunkadunk" (1) is similar to Meredith's in that the soundwork initially suggests a poem quite different from the one that yields after multiple readings. The poem cannot be paraphrased, but it tracks an experience of being overwhelmed by shock and frustration.

The poem is driven by soundwork. A short "u" sounds forms a kind of engine that drives the poem forward. The first line has five stresses, each coinciding with a short "u"—making the five short "u"s dominate the line, and giving the line a tripping, speedy motion, and reversing the lineage of Western prosody, where the stressed syllables of English meter correspond to the long syllables of the prosody of Ancient Greek and Latin. The rat-a-tat-tat of the opening line speeds the reader along on heavy stresses of short duration. The second line, has six short "u" sounds—but this time with multiple caesuras through the line, recreating the same pattern of the first, but slowed by the period and the commas. In the third line, a long "e" begins to join the short "u," gaining momentum until finally the engine changes to long "o" sounds in the final lines. The "u" sound recedes—there are three in the third line, four in the fourth line, two in the fifth line, and then only one in the sixth line. But the "u" returns in line 7, with two to three short "u"s in the remaining lines, until the fourteenth line has none at all. "P," "k," and "s" sounds dominate the poem and provide another form of sonic through-line. The soundwork is hypnotic, the repetitions aided by the frequent use of noun phrases rather than sentences, with syntax often stuck at the nominal level. At times, I feel myself tripping on the unstressed prepositions, and trying to keep up with the staccato rhythms of a word like "badunkadunk." I often have the experience, when first reading a poem, of only hearing the rhythms and sounds, and having to go back for sense in later readings— which can make reading a book of poems time consuming. In this case, I was so transfixed by the sound, I wasn't sure I even wanted a meaning. If this were a nonsense poem, I would quite happily return to it for snippets of meaning and rhythmic pleasure.

But, of course, the poem does have a clear semantic meaning, and it is about Trump. The poem opens with the president's tendency to assault and harass the women in his proximity and how it is unfathomable to many of us that this behavior is not only continuous and brazen, but actually part of his brand. He might seem impossible—his brazen, thin-skinned, and racist behavior would be unthinkable for any other politician—and yet this knowledge does us no good. We watch in shock as his brazen disregard for anything like decency succeeds over and over on the national and world stages.

The poem doesn't hinge or turn. In the second line the behavior "stumps us." In the final lines we remained stumped, though the verb "stumps" returns as a play on "stub"—"The umpteenth boast / Stumps our toe." The body is present in the poem, invoking the women being grabbed, Trump's wandering hands, and then in our bodies, "our elbows

& eyeballs," as we witness the spectacle. And again, one could make the argument that the poem hinges at the couplet, when the focus of the poem switches from the unnamed aggressor's physical body to the body politic's frustration with the bodily desire of our elected leader, but this feels like a forced turn—after all, "us" is present in the second line. The bodily witness we bear is present from the first sentence of the poem.

The poem's syntax is also almost entirely enjambed. Of the fifteen periods in the poem, only four appear at the end of the line, and there are only four verbs acting as verbs in the entire poem—"pumps" in the third line, and "stumps" in the second line, and then again "stumps" twice in the thirteenth line. I'm not counting "Believe" because it is a quoted phrase, rather than acting as an action verb in the poem. Note that the opening verb, "stump," returns twice more at the end of the poem, and with the same object—us. The *we* of the poem is stable from start to finish, acted upon by the litany of bad behavior. Most of the poem is composed of noun phrases, accumulating as outrages, with the only action being the befouling of our air with a "funky rumble" and our own injury and confusion that blend "stump" with the more expected "stub"—bringing our gobsmacked outrage into the space of physical pain. The body of the predator is described in staccato short vowels; our own shock arrives in four monosyllabic interjections, slowing the poem in the final line.

In playing out the befuddlement that many of us have felt in the face of Trump's behavior, and of his successes in spite of it, the poem begins in incomprehension and ends there. The poem is a spiral staircase of disbelief and outrage at the outrageous, and the poem intensifies and literalizes as it moves forward. It doesn't turn in the traditional sense, it clarifies and emphasizes. It runs in place. Like Alvarez's list poem, the motion of the poem tumbles forward with addition, but unlike Alvarez, the turn is not back onto the douzaine in a sense of hinging back. Rather, Hayes intensifies the movement by resisting the forward trajectory of syntax, accumulating noun phrases that ultimately act on us throughout the piece. The book itself has a similar arc—the sonnets in sequence do not tell a story as much as they trace an awareness that grows and intensifies as it moves from poem to poem.

The final poem that I will consider is Danez Smith's "it began right here," from their landmark collection *Don't Call Us Dead*. The book as a whole grapples with testing positive for HIV and having been infected with the virus; this particular sonnet precedes a crown of sonnets about the diagnosis.

The poem begins with the moment of infection, and the sublime of sexuality, the "monster" signaling the change in identity marked by sexuality—as Eve Sedgwick put it, "sexual desire is an unpredictably powerful solvent of stable identities" (85)—before the virus becomes a kind of monster that his body harbors, as well as a metonym for the infecting lover. The title of the poem suggests an entry into narrative, and there is a story—but the events are looping, and the realizations reflective and meditative, rather than chronological or unfolding. We don't move from start to finish, but from origin to meaning, to the way that the event spirals back onto itself, resisting chronology in that the single event persists as a kind of indelible image or a kind of haunting. The syntax is choppy, a kind of syncopated push and pull against the usual rhythms of hypotaxis or parataxis. The lowercase letters resist the sentence boundaries, as does the frequent beginning of sentences with conjunctions, as well as the starting and stopping of sentences in the middle of the line and the use of colons. The poem is a study in pacing—and I think that my intuitive sense that the poem spirals rather than hinges is based on the pacing and how it crosses the boundaries of pacing usually provided by the line, the period, and the comma. If the minimal requirements of the English sentence are a subject, a verb, and a complete thought, Smith seems to engage fragmentation in order to destabilize the coherency of the sentence. They begin with a sentence fragment, "a humbling at my knees," before using that setting to explore the inciting event. Then "me" followed by a colon—the pronoun to be explained by a sentence—and "him" followed by a colon, repeating the pattern.

It is worth paying attention to the the syntax's relationship to the line. Periods and commas often place pauses into the line, while the line breaks are often enjambed against syntax—syncopating the line and the movement of the poem. The first line breaks an infinitive! This is highly inadvisable in most cases, and yet here it preserves the openness of "wanted to" before landing on "watch." The next line break comes between the object of the sentence "me" and the prepositional phrase introducing the predatory allegory. The next line break cuts the verb "keeps" from the participle "dying"—transforming "keeps" into an auxiliary verb rather than a transitive verb—again retaining the sense of "keeps" as "holding."

"The devil" is a subject that begins the next sentence but is then cut from "sleeps"—and only in that fifth line do we arrive at an end-stopped line ending. As the poem moves forward, the end of the line is more likely to coincide with a syntactical ending, but the sense of flux, once established, continues through the poem.

The poem also makes the body into a landscape. The first two lines suggest the expected boundaries of two people with two bodies, but in the third line the body becomes both carrion in the desert and the desert itself—"vultures grazing my veins." The self is found in the cataloging of its parts, becoming at times shrunk smaller than those parts ("i will die in this bloodcell") and at times growing past the boundaries of the body ("i am a house"). The movement of scale between the metonymic reduction and expansive landscape gives a sense of how the poem doesn't move in a single direction or hinge from one understanding of the self to another understanding of the self, but rather lets the self pulse with meaning.

Events echo out across time, reverberating rather than resolving, and ghosting the landscape rather than restructuring it. In this poem, there is a motion toward the completeness or wholeness of the self, but in response to the way in the which the self was shattered in the opening, so it is not a clear movement from wounding to healing or fear to acceptance. Rather, all aspects of the infection and its ramifications seem omnipresent, time rendered flat rather than linear. That circular trajectory loops back on itself, so that the consciousness of the poem is simultaneously retroactive and forward-moving. The poem doesn't hinge, it pulses; it resists resolution, and in part I chose this poem because it opens onto a crown of sonnets. So in its final moments the poem is bridging to a larger sequence, rather than resolving something. In the same way that the eccentric syntax and orthography resist the typical boundings of sentences by engaging the rules in unexpected ways, the poem engages the motion of the sonnet but uses the template while moving in unexpected ways. Again, I think the poem intensifies rather than turns.

I do think, to return to Oppenheimer and Levin's argument about the sonnet embodying the divided self of modern subjectivity, that Smith is capturing the divided self in this poem. The speaker observes himself and experiences himself. The metaphors don't turn to allegory, and the division between living and dying is a tension within the speaker. But that tension is not presented in one way to be turned over and seen another way. Rather, that tension carries out across the poem—it opens up in the beginning and remains open through the end. The definitional concern of the sonnet is still acted out, but with the division omnipresent rather than revealed through presenting one side and then another side.

The poem does move toward acceptance, but it also hovers in place, the final line returning us to the opening of the poem, "where it happened is where i sleep." And I would argue that the speaker is not enacting the process of coming to an understanding, but rather enacting the experience of having arrived at an understanding that is not static. This distinction is central to my argument—that we are used to sonnets that show us a mind moving from one point to another, and that this poem, like a cubist painting showing all the angles at once, is presenting the unsettled nature of an unstable acceptance, not the flux of moving from one point to another, but the flux of where one is, which is typically not thought of as a form of flux at all—and that is precisely the thing that the sonnet can do that I didn't know it could do.

This is a very small selection of sonnets, and my goal is not to discount the turn or volta, but rather to show another way that the sonnet might move forward. The sonnet is a highly cathected form in English. The sonnet always seems on its way out and always on its way back in. Mastering the sonnet is often a kind of Everest for poets, but many poets regard the sonnet as code for a kind of conservative formalism or an entry to an exclusive club. Eavan Boland writes of her initial resistance to the sonnet, "I had read it as school and resisted writing it," because she found the sonnet "too finished to ever find the new beginning in the literature I was trying to find" (43–44). She even goes so far as to call the form "a sideshow of empire," before discovering Patrick Kavanagh's sonnet "Epic," which showed her that "a great form can discover a poet just as much and as often as a poet discovers a form" (45). Resistance to the sonnet usually shows up in the writing of writers who have since embraced the form. I set out to consider the ways that sonnets turn in order to provide a few techniques I might offer you as writers—paradigms and templates that you could occupy rhetorically, the same way you might occupy a rhyme scheme. What I found was a movement for sonnets that had been hiding in plain sight. Not surprisingly, as I began to look for the turn in a few of my favorite sonnets, I found a helix instead—a spiral staircase that turns around a central concern or concerns, emphasizing and deepening a single problem. So instead, here is an unexpected paradigm, a sonnet that need not turn, but rather intensify.

I am excited by this development, because it suggests that the argument I have been making through a number of essays—largely that the teaching of form requires attending to the rhetorical demand of each form—is not untrue, exactly, but is limited. It's a bit of a truism that if you give artists rules, the first thing they will do is figure out how to break them. I've always hated the euphemism "works"—meaning, "I liked it despite its having violated my expectations of the rules of a particular genre"—because it often feels like the end of a discussion, rather than the reopening of what is possible and impossible in art. Somewhere in Aristotle's *Poetics*, he points out that we could just slosh around a bunch of paint on a canvas, but we wouldn't like it, and it wouldn't be art. But, obviously, the entire abstract expressionist movement did just that, and we do like it, but they had Clement Greenberg there to tell everyone *why* to like it. So in my reconsideration of sonnets, I hope not to abandon a traditional view of the sonnet, but rather to expand our understanding of how sonnets might work and to suggest that one thing may hide another, and that as writers our perceptions must be honed to a keen edge.

A Postscript

There is another argument underneath my argument—which is that if the sonnet is sign or symptom of a certain kind of subjectivity, of an experience of the self that is distinctly Western, goes by the name of modernism, and is defined by the division of the self, then to find another motion for the sonnet—one that is not centrally divided between one thing and another, but spins out over a central concern—suggests to me that another way of being is arriving or has arrived. My argument may suggest a new development in the history of subjectivity that future scholars might find themselves tracking, and if past is prologue, the archive of the human will be found in poems.

A Personal Note

When I moved to New York to attend New York University's MFA program in 1999, I had the good fortune to become Phillis Levin's assistant on her groundbreaking anthology, *The Penguin Book of the Sonnet: 500 Years of a Classic Tradition in English*, published in 2001. I cannot recommend Levin's extensive introduction to this volume highly enough. It is an indispensable source for anyone seeking to understand the development of the sonnet and its role in literary history.

Nothing has ever been more educational for me than watching her assemble this anthology and craft its introduction through multiple stages of development and revision. Many of the sources I have cited are the direct or indirect result of her work. Perhaps no one can ever sufficiently acknowledge a mentor's role in the shaping of one's thinking, but here I want to recognize how significantly my understanding of the sonnet has been shaped by the generosity and erudition of Phillis Levin.

Notes

1. I use the word "embodiment" as a slightly loaded term, and one that indexes my debt to Arthur Danto's philosophical definition of art: "To be a work of art is to be (i) *about* something and (ii) to *embody its meaning*" (Danto 195, italics in original). My own attachment to the notion of *embodiment* is that it is the concept wherein I locate the membrane between art and life, and I am highly critical of art movements or philosophies that do not respect the distinction between the art that "embodies" something and the "something" from life that is being embodied.

2. While it's not crucial to my argument, this is literally true. *Hamlet* was first performed in 1609, the same year that Shakespeare's sonnets were published.

3. When I teach this poem to undergraduates, they are rarely familiar with even a few of the atrocities listed. I will often start a class by assigning each letter to a student, who then uses their phone to research the event referenced. After we have gone around the room with each student reporting back on their assigned letter, we return to the poem with its full horror restored through shared research.

On another note, I have been less successful at convincing students of the precise irony of "Let's make a modern primer for our kids" and will often receive a few papers during the semester about how Julia Alvarez is somewhat perverse in her desire to teach children the alphabet through atrocity. I've tried to explain that embodied in the poem is the idea that we ought to live up to the self we try to present to children—we would definitely not go to kindergarten classes with pictures of Auschwitz—but irony requires a shared understanding that is often unavailable to people who are new to a particular discursive community.

4. My go-to example of a poem that distracts through form is this epigram from W. H. Auden's "Shorts":

Let us honor if we can
The vertical man,
Though we value none
But the horizontal one.

(53)

Read one way, it's about trying to value the living and not valorizing the dead. On the other hand, well, put your own mind in the gutter (it's the best place from which to gaze at the stars!).

5. For a more in depth exploration of the multiple uses of the second person in literature, see my essay "Ambiguities of the Second Person in English Language Poetry and Fiction" in the March/April 2024 edition of *American Poetry Review*.

Works Cited

Alvarez, Julia. "33." In *Homecoming*, pp. 57–102. Plume, 1984.

Auden, W. H. "Shorts." *Collected Poems*. Edited by Edward Mendelson. Vintage, 1991.

Boland, Eavan. "Discovering the Sonnet." In *The Making of a Sonnet: A Norton Anthology*, edited by Edward Hirsch and Eavan Boland, pp. 43–48. Norton, 2008.

Chaucer, Geoffrey. "Canticus Troili." In *The Penguin Book of the Sonnet*, edited by Phillis Levin, p. lxxvii. Penguin, 2001.

Cunningham, J. V. "The Problem of Form." In *Praising It New: The Best of the New Criticism*, edited by Garrick Davis, pp. 220–23. Swallow Press, 2008.

Danto, Arthur. *After the End of Art*. Princeton University Press, 2007.

Hayes, Terrance. *American Sonnets for My Past and Future Assassin*. Penguin, 2018.

Levin, Phillis. "Introduction." In *The Penguin Book of the Sonnet*, edited by Phillis Levin, pp. xxxvii–lxxiv. Penguin, 2001.

Meredith, William. "The Illiterate." In *Effort at Speech*, p. 40. Triquarterly Books, 1997.

Merrill, James. "The Book of Ephraim." In *The Changing Light at Sandover*, edited by J. D. McClatchy and Stephen Yenser, pp. 1–92. Knopf, 2006.

Oppenheimer, Paul. *The Birth of the Modern Mind: Self, Consciousness, and the Invention of the Sonnet*. Oxford University Press, 1989.

Pinsky, Robert. "ABC." In *Jersey Rain*, p. 10. FSG, 2000.

Sedgwick, Eve. *Epistemology of the Closet*. University of California Press, 1990.

Smith, Danez. *Don't Call Us Dead*. Graywolf, 2017.

Further Reading

Boland, Eavan and Edward Hirsch, eds. *The Making of a Sonnet: A Norton Anthology.* Norton, 2008.

Burt, Stephanie and David Mikics, eds. *The Art of the Sonnet.* Belknap, 2010.

Fuller, John. *The Oxford Book of Sonnets.* Oxford University Press, 2000.

Hollander, John. *Rhyme's Reason: A Guide to English Verse,* 4th ed. Yale University Press, 2014.

Levin, Phillis, ed. *The Penguin Book of the Sonnet.* Penguin, 2001.

I Thought I Hated Inaugural Poems
(But It Turns Out I Don't)

Humiliation, 2009

On January 20th, 2009, Barack Obama was inaugurated as president. Obama had inspired artists and intellectuals in a way that I had never seen before. As a poet, I was hoping that there would be an inaugural poem, and yes, as a snob, I was hoping that it would neither be neither a slam poet nor a new formalist. I wanted someone whose work I respect—someone whose work is lyric rather than partisan; who teaches, rather than proselytizes; an artist in the modernist tradition, rather than an entertainer with a book of rhymes. I wanted an adult who writes for other adults with an intuitive sense of what I mean by the word "adult."

When Obama announced Elizabeth Alexander as his inaugural poet, I was thrilled. I loved *American Sublime*, and her publisher, Graywolf, is my dream press. I liked her personal connection to Obama. I saw in her the hope that somewhere at the colleges I have worked, I might rub shoulders with someone who would turn out to be president. I *identify* with Alexander. Yes, this is an aspirational identification. She has tenure at an Ivy League school, a loyal and well-regarded press, and a significant readership—all things I can only envy. But in the penumbra of the Obama flame, wasn't hope itself a form of aspirational identification?

When the day arrived, I eagerly sat in front of the TV. I couldn't wait to see what Michelle Obama was wearing. I had loved her outfits through the campaign. I have an entirely un-ironic love for the first couple. I literally swooned over Barack Obama's description of their courtship in *The Audacity of Hope*. Their victory fist bump was the most genuine moment of affection I have ever seen between a politician and his partner. It almost healed the trauma I still feel from having witnessed the consumingly open-mouthed kiss that Al Gore gave Tipper in 2000. I wanted to bathe in the reflected glow of the Obamas' affection and triumph. After six years of anger and two years of anxiety, a day of unadulterated happiness hardly seemed too much to ask.

And I had helped. I was part of his victory. I had knocked on doors. I had taken early morning carpools to Philadelphia to do campaign work. I had registered voters. This was my inauguration. My liberal heart had liberally thrilled to the strains of Jon Bon Jovi and Bettye LaVette singing "A Change Is Gonna Come" the day before. Fine, Rick Warren was giving the invocation—but even Obama's magnanimous reach across the partisan aisle gave off warm fuzzies.

The day of the inauguration, I sat glued to my TV. I had no interest in braving the cold and actually going to Washington. I hadn't had quite this feeling since the wedding of Charles and Diana. John Roberts fumbled the oath. Obama's speech was wonderfully calibrated. Yo-Yo Ma and Itzhak Perlman gave a riveting performance. Aretha Franklin sang "My Country, 'Tis of Thee" and I loved her hat. Then the finale: Elizabeth Alexander and the inaugural poem. I may never have anticipated a poem so much.

But as Alexander took to the podium, the camera cut to the audience. These dedicated souls, who had braved freezing temperatures to see the president take the oath of office, were leaving. They were getting up and leaving. En masse. Some stations actually stopped their coverage after Franklin had finished. We had worked so hard for this day. *I* had worked hard for this day. And there, at the end of it, were people walking away from the art form I love. There stood poetry where it always seems to stand. Ignored. Humiliated. Abandoned.

Robert Frost, 1961

I've never really been able to warm up to Robert Frost. Certainly, "Stopping by Woods on a Snowy Evening" has the amazing talent of memorizing itself into your brain, but I've always found "The Road Not Taken" about as endearing as head lice. My educational experience has always presented Frost in one of two lights. Either he is the charming New England curmudgeon—hardworking, honest, straightforward—or he is the sly parodist, playing at Northeastern grit while winking at the careful reader. Jay Parini's biography of Frost contains the following index entries under "public persona": "interferes with inner poet," "mode perfected," "vs. private, gap widens in late 1920s and 1930s," "Yankee voice, worn as mask." To all of these, I say, "No, thank you."

Frost was the face of American poetry, and in many ways, he still is. It may seem odd that Frost was the first poet to give an inaugural poem, given poetry's centrality to America's previous century, but it was actually the disappearance of poetry from public life that motivated Kennedy to ask Frost. According to William Meredith, an inaugural poem "was a novel idea, and one that focused attention on Kennedy as a man of culture, as a man interested in culture." It was precisely that movement of poetry out of the mainstream—a movement that had taken place a good six decades prior—that set the stage for Kennedy to look cultured by appreciating poetry.

I've often wondered how much Frost is responsible for the box in which most Americans seem to keep poetry. "The Road Not Taken" was actually printed in full on the cover of my high school yearbook and it seems to embody all the attitudes towards poetry that I hate: sentimental, nostalgic, trivial. Of course, the real Frost was none of these things. Lionel Trilling, when speaking in honor of Frost in 1959, said, "I have to say that my Frost . . . is not the Frost existing in the minds of so many of his admirers. . . . He is not the Frost who reassures us by his affirmations of old virtues, simplicities, pieties, and ways of feeling. . . . I regard Robert Frost as a terrifying poet."

The next year, Kennedy did not ask Frost for an inaugural poem, but rather specified the poem that he wanted Frost to read. Frost, however, did write another poem to introduce that poem (after he had been firmly told that he could not give an unscripted introduction). The introductory poem proved impossible to read, as the cold was making Frost's eyes tear up, and "The Gift Outright" was read to the gathering from Frost's memory.

When I was beginning this essay, I read "The Gift Outright" to my husband. The poem begins "The land was ours before we were the land's." The poem explores the transition from colonization to belonging to the landscape. "Oh my God," I said to my husband, "did he just celebrate genocide?" My husband responded with the suggestion that I might be engaging in a less-than-nuanced reading of the poem.

Parini points out that the poem might "seem horribly chauvinistic, even belligerent . . . Frost's poem ignored the Native American angle all together," although Parini means that Frost ignored their perspective, rather than their existence. The poem says that "The deed of gift was many deeds of war." I find it hard to believe that this is simply war with European powers.

The poem ultimately suggests a form of pathology—a poem is always ironic, with layers of perspective and understanding mediating against any sort of simplistic "meaning." Of course, this is wonderful for those of us who want to represent the world in its complexity—and awful for those of us who are the objects of simplifying critics. I've ultimately come to find the poem a compelling treatise on how one might understand the horror of the history that is in many ways the history of mankind. Territory has never been easily taken or easily held. That Americans "forthwith found salvation in surrender" strikes me as the sort of surrender that an alcoholic makes to alcohol (or more salutarily, to a higher power). Frost's surrender is to violence and democracy.

As a military brat and a Jew, I was raised to believe in America as an ideal rather than a place. Because my homes were arbitrary and changing, I could never quite understand attachment to place—there were lots of places, and they weren't that different. But the texts that formed my life seemed necessary and specific. The Old Testament and the Constitution are not replaceable. In fact, I loved the way that the Constitution grew out of the failed Articles of Confederation, as well as the way that the amendments allowed for those ideals to be tempered and adjusted.

Frost's poem ultimately serves as a powerful corrective to my deracinated and modular idea of America. It insists on the violence of displacement and the violences—both physical and emotional—which are embedded in the achievement of statehood. The final couplet ultimately seems to me to speak of how we tell ourselves a story of sui generis emergence, even when we know it to be false:

But still unstoried, artless, unenhanced,
Such as she was, such as she would become.

Certainly, this suggests a blank slate for the colonials to start with—but it also suggests the violence of erasure. Not "storyless" but "unstoried." The stories are being removed, and carefully displaced to make room for us—or the *us* to whom we trace ourselves.

When I first started with Frost, I felt like his poem was itself an erasure of America's violent past, but I've come to feel it as a careful exploration of the perspective that condoned and embraced that violence.

Maya Angelou, 1993

When I think of Maya Angelou, I actually think of David Alan Grier doing Maya Angelou on *Saturday Night Live*. ("Don't a lay a finger on myyyyyyy but-tah-fin-gah!") Since I was born after Angelou's most significant political and theatrical achievements, her persona far outweighs her accomplishments in my consciousness.

One hesitates to say too loudly that one does not like Maya Angelou's poetry. In some circles, it goes without saying—you simply walk into a faculty lounge and bemoan the fact that the only poem your students have ever heard is "Still I Rise." Harold Bloom wrote, "Her poetry has a large public, but very little critical esteem. It . . . makes no formal or cognitive demands upon the reader." *Library Journal* assessed her first volume of poetry as "well done schlock poetry, not to be confused with poetry for people who read poetry."

But in other circles, Maya Angelou is the quintessential role model. She embodies the major themes that preoccupied twentieth-century America: (1) overcoming adversity, (2) making victimhood a position of strength, and (3) celebrating one's heritage. At a moment when many writers were focused on the impossibility of communication through language, Angelou was focused on making her own letters crystal clear—and it won her an audience that included President Clinton.

While I tend not to think of Frost and Angelou as having much in common, Angelou's inaugural poem "On the Pulse of Morning" contains multiple echoes of "The Gift Outright." Like Frost, Angelou gives the land a seductive agency, insisting that the inhabitants of America inhabit her. She opens with the landscape, but ultimately reveals that her poem is in the voice of that landscape:

I am that Tree planted by the River,
Which will not be moved.

I, the Rock, I, the River, I, the Tree,
I am yours—your passages have been paid.

Angelou does cast a wider net than Frost. She lists multiple peoples, making the country speak to a veritable laundry list of heritages and identities, including sexual orientation and economic privilege in her list. While Frost began with the arrival of the colonists, Angelou goes all the way back to the Jurassic period, remembering even "the dinosaur, who left dried tokens / Of their sojourn here / On our planet floor."

When Toni Morrison called Bill Clinton the first Black president, she did not mean that he was somehow in tune with Black culture. (Ask Sistah Souljah about that one.) She meant that his body had become subject to the kind of hostile surveillance and judgment to which Black bodies have long been subjected. So perhaps Angelou was the ideal poet to inaugurate Bill Clinton in that she had dedicated her life to pushing back against the racism that subjugated American Blacks. In fact, Angelou left America entirely, living in Ghana until Malcolm X inspired her to return.

I don't remember the poem from the inauguration, but I do read it every year. It's in the High Holiday Prayer Book of the Reconstructionist Movement (a branch of Judaism), and I always look forward to reading it. The ending always moves me:

Here, on the pulse of this new day,
You may have the grace to look up and out
And into your sister's eyes,
And into your brother's face,
Your country,
And say simply
Very simply
With hope—
Good morning.

I spend a lot of my time explaining why I love certain poems, but the best poems catch you off guard. The best art simply floors you, and that "Good morning" always floors me. The build to it seems so rhetorically inflated, and the poem includes the sort of lists that usually make me cringe. But the closing is almost like those Beach Boys harmonies that are so sweet they hurt more than cacophony; the plain-spoken turns into a quotation of itself, unmooring the simplicity of the simple.

The frustration that critics express over Angelou's mostly dreadful poetry is that the poetry feels like pandering and weighs down an otherwise celebrated body of work. But on January 20, 1993, faced with the largest audience of her life, Angelou delivered a poem that at least this reader of poetry cannot help but admire.

Miller Williams, 1997

It seems almost fitting that I have next to nothing to say about the poem written for Clinton's second inaugural. It was an awkward time. On one hand, it's embarrassing how much time we spent worrying about frivolous things. On the other hand, I think we'd all be thrilled to exchange concerns over the impending collapse of the Euro for concerns over precisely what would constitute sex with Monica Lewinsky. I have the same feeling about Clinton's second term as I do about the time I spent reading *Atlas Shrugged*: what a lot of *sturm und drang* over nothing.

Williams's "Of History and Hope" seems a little more ponderous and a little more obvious than its peers. It rests on the image of the children who will inherit the future (as though they aren't here now). It feels pedantic. It opens, "We have memorized America, / how it was born and who we have been and where." It sounds like someone ran the prompt from an AP American History exam though Google Translate and back again. At a certain point it resolves into rhyme. The syntax slides from sentence to nominal phrases and then past the point of coherence. The results are less than sanguine:

But how do we fashion the future? Who can say how
except in the minds of those who will call it Now?
The children. The children. And how does our garden grow?
With waving hands—oh, rarely in a row—
And flowering faces. And brambles, that we can no longer allow.

Yes, "Now" is capitalized in the original. I'm not sure if that's because you should say it a little louder than the other words, or if it's because it's a proper name when the children call it. I sort of like the leap to lines from a nursery rhyme, but the landing leaves me entirely confused. Are the children the flowering faces? What are the brambles? Why can't they be allowed? Why start two sentences with conjunctions?

The ending is more pedantic than the beginning, bringing the strong wisdom that history is important:

If we can truly remember, they will not forget.

I don't think that's true at all, but even that aside, the poem just feels flat. Maybe inaugural poems are only a good idea for a first term. Or maybe it underscores the wisdom of Kennedy asking for a specific Frost poem, rather than commissioning an inaugural poem. After all, Clinton used "Don't Stop" for his theme song. He didn't commission Fleetwood Mac for an original composition.

Elizabeth Alexander, 2009

Adding to the painful humiliation of America essentially walking away before the inaugural poem was read was that, at least initially, I didn't like the poem, and neither did anyone I knew.

My non-poet friends started calling me the day after the inauguration to ask the same question: Was Elizabeth Alexander's poem as bad as they had thought? Grudgingly, I felt that I had to confirm that it was. The inaugural poem had broken one of the central tenets of good poems. It had too many things at stake. Instead of focusing on a single consciousness, it had spread itself too thin. The *New York Times* published a transcript of the poem that butchered the lines. When I spoke to other poets, there was almost no love for the poem. We all agreed that it was clumsy and diffuse—that it was trying to appeal to a wider audience that doesn't exist.

When I started this essay, I had planned on discussing how Alexander's brilliant characterizations in her other works are dissipated by her introduction of multiple subjectivities. But I don't think that anymore. I've come to respect "Praise Song for the Day" as a poem. With each reread, I find the poem feels wiser and wiser. On the morning of the inauguration, it felt obvious. Even the name felt less like a title, and more like the description of her commission. But over time, and away from the initial occasion, it becomes more and more the poem I need.

I think that the poem is about the difficulty of joy in the face of history's weight. It opens on to the conflict between community and isolation:

Each day we go about our business,
walking past each other, catching each other's
eyes or not, about to speak or something.

I did not realize how much this captured what I've come to feel about democracy—how we have to speak to each other, and yet we don't—though for very good reasons. A later line says that we have "each / one of our ancestors on our tongues," recognizing that to start the conversation we need to have might be to fight or entrench. Our heritage is always with us, and our grievances are real.

The poem tends to slip away to individual scenes.

Someone is stitching up a hem, darning
a hole in a uniform, patching a tire,
repairing things in need of repair.

The images focus on brokenness. The poem is about effort, not achievement; the progressive tense, not the perfect. "Someone is trying to make music"—the music never arrives. People wait, people begin, but there is no conclusion, no triumph, no reward. "We need to find a place where we are safe."

At the time, I thought this was placing the emphasis on America's promise, rather than America's reality. But I think this was because I didn't want the inauguration to be a beginning—I wanted it to be the victory. I wanted to feel finished—to let Obama work his magic. Alexander's focus on process was ultimately prescient. The poem says, "we encounter each other in words" and what felt truistic in 2009 (and still feels a touch flat) feels more complicated in 2012. Our words are failing—but we can't stop talking.

The poem ultimately embraces love as the necessary mode for connection. "What if the mightiest word is love?" the poem asks. This is an easy line to ridicule, and certainly I did. But this is the problem of all liberals. Conservatives can find consistency in their positions, as can radicals. But for the liberal—and I used Hayden White's definition here—as one who believes that the world should be improved upon rather than remade or preserved—it is love that keeps us from revolution while insisting on change.

The poem embraces the light of love and concludes "praise song for walking forward in that light." I tend to prefer sentences rather than nominal phrases, but in the nostalgia for the hope I felt that morning, this seems like the right ending. A fantasy lets us imagine arriving at a goal without the humiliation, setbacks, and failures that actual work entails. I wanted a fantasy. Now that we've endured humiliations, setbacks, and failures, "Praise Song for the Day" feels less mawkish.

In the entire inaugural ceremony, there were only three original components—which is to say, three pieces composed solely for that day. The oath that John Roberts administered was the same oath every president takes, even if most presidents don't need a do-over. The music performed by Perlman, Ma, and Franklin were all familiar pieces. Only Obama's speech, Warren's invocation, and Alexander's poem were composed for that day. All three of these new texts straddled the line between art and lecture. Perhaps an inaugural poem can only be evaluated from the other side of a presidency, and it's unfair to ask it to be evaluated too soon. "My Country, 'Tis of Thee" has had over two hundred years for us to warm up to it. Why should "Praise Song for the Day" not get a couple of years?

Craft vs. Authenticity

Americans love authenticity. Authenticity, loosely defined, is the belief that any given performance matches the internal essence of the performer. Of course, this is impossible. Just as one modulates one's speech around one's mother differently than around one's lover, all action and all speech are modulated to fit the parties present. This is the central insight of Martin Buber's *Ich und Du*, and precisely the complication of identity that Judith Butler has spent a career exploring. One approaches authenticity asymptotically, not directly. I return frequently to this sentence from Auden's, "Words and the Word": "When we genuinely speak, we do not have the words ready to do our bidding; we have to find them, and we do not know exactly what we are going to say until we have said it, and we say and hear something new that has never been said or heard before"

(105). Authenticity—in this case—involves surprise. It lies in the process, not the performance.

Of course, this desire for authenticity drives us to odd places. Reality television draws huge audiences as we see "real people" undergoing "real emotion." But what of the fact that almost no one who has their house made over is actually able to live in that house? The taxes are so high that almost every "winner" has to sell the house you were so excited about them getting to inhabit. *Dateline NBC* fabricated underaged sirens to draw out pedophiles, until the suicide of one forced the conclusion of the series. The basic structures of most reality television contests involve isolation from friends and family, sleep deprivation, overexertion, humiliation, constant berating—all diluted versions of the tools familiar to interrogators and torturers.

The thrill of the authentic is even kept in place when it is revealed to be falsified, because the outrage we feel *is* authentic. The goal of the audience is to be moved—to experience something that creates emotion—but safely. The "reaction video" is a curious phenomenon of our lust for authenticity—forcing the audience to become the performer. A YouTube search for "two girls one cup reaction" brings up close to 20,000 hits—which means that roughly 20,000 people across the country turned the authentic disgust of a friend or relative into a performance for strangers. And the more uncomfortable the reaction, the better.

But our love of the authentic makes us easily fooled by craft. Think of Idris Elba auditioning to play a Baltimore thug-cum-businessman in *The Wire*. He withheld his British identity, and his crafted accent got him the part precisely because David Simon didn't know he wasn't from Baltimore (Rose, n.p.). The rise of reality television indexes an odd flip by which politics became entertainment, and entertainment became politics. Americans love the use of "actual people," despite the fact that we've never quite believed that actors or politicians are indeed actual people. We can't get enough of things being ripped from the headlines, and the balm of "but this really happened" has long been used to justify our most prurient interest in true crime novels and sensational television dramas. As U2 put it, our love of authenticity means that we often prefer that which is "even better than the real thing."

In addition to being fooled by crafted performances that pass for authentically true, we often embrace authenticity in a way that is bound to disappoint. Think Joe the Plumber, or Hank Williams, Jr. There are certain personas, like J. D. Salinger, or Harper Lee, who know the premium that has been placed on their authenticity and therefore become recluses. Did they keep silent in order to avoid becoming spokespersons? Or did they keep silent so that the authenticity of their work would go unquestioned? Like children watching a horror movie, most of us want to see at a remove what we hope will never happen in our own lives.

In America, the fame artists—those artists who are especially good at being famous (think Andy Warhol, Madonna, Paris Hilton) are especially good at a kind of "authentic performativity." In *Truth or Dare*, Warren Beatty asks rhetorically why Madonna would do anything off camera. He seems aware that her fame is fundamentally misaligned with his. Not that he doesn't love being famous, but he has a line of privacy that he keeps an authentic self on one side of. But Angelou and Frost may be more aligned with Madonna, and Alexander more aligned with Beatty. It's the ability to fake authenticity that makes for good occasional poems.

Angelou and Frost also had significant political involvements. It should be no surprise that the best inaugural poems are from Maya Angelou and Robert Frost. These are two poets with a clear understanding of what it takes to become famous and what it means to stay famous, as well as what it means to act on a world stage. The Latin proverb says that art has no enemy but ignorance. Ignorance may just be politics' best friend. Is it any surprise that it's hard to get art and politics together?

What Should an Inaugural Poem Be?

I began this essay not to praise inaugural poems, but to damn them. I thought I had hated the inaugural poems, and wanted to figure out a) what I wanted from them and b) why they hadn't delivered.

But living with these poems, I've found more and more to admire. We repeat to ourselves over and over that we live in highly polarized times, though it does seem odd that we have to keep repeating it. The repetition compulsion of the twenty-four-hour news cycle might be a sign of the death drive. Should an inaugural poem capture America? Which America? To quote Langston Hughes, "America never was America to me." Each of these inaugural poems look at the America that's all of America—even when it fails to live up to the promises that we like to call "America," and especially when we remember the sheer expanse of violence on which our nation was built. As Langston Hughes writes later in that poem, "And yet I swear this oath—America will be!" If inaugurals are about aspirations for an ideal presidency, they must also present an aspirational vision for the country.

For me, the most painful aspect of democracy is the recognition that I cannot disavow what I find distasteful. When I am surprised or bothered by a political action or protest, I have to remember that we are of the same nation. The anti-intellectualism that permeates American politics is impossible for me to disavow. Some days it feels like living in an abusive marriage where divorce is impossible—but the solution is not to fantasize about divorce. It's to take counteraction. As long as I believe in democracy, I must believe that the voices of the ignorant, the uninformed, and the hateful are necessary voices. But of course, to respond to those voices is exhausting. And responding to any voices on their own terms can often endorse them. The media's criticism of the "Occupy" movements was that they had no demands—but that criticism was also a form of fascination that the occupiers turned into airtime. In trying to understand their "missing" demands, the media endorsed the movements by allowing them to shift the national conversation.

I once shocked a class of students by telling them that they weren't entitled to their opinion—that opinions had to be earned and supported by evidence. I suggested that they try to replace the word "opinion" with "informed judgment." One of the students responded, "But not on the street! Not in the voting booth!" And I responded that as much as I believed that my pedagogy mattered to their entire lives, yes, they were free to do as they liked in the voting booth. My insistence on "informed judgment" reached only as far as the walls of the classroom and the grade on their transcript. The student reminded me precisely how limited my power was—how limited any educator's power is—which is, I think, a hallmark of democratic society.

In the early years of Gulf War II, one of my professors insisted that "Not in My Name" was an impossible/illegitimate elocution in a democracy. The refusal to endorse the war that the phrase captures was clear—but it's a fantasy. To be a citizen in a democracy is to recognize how clearly implicated we are in each other's actions. Barack Obama's 2008 lecture on race discussed how we can never turn our back on our community or our nation without turning our back on ourselves. Theresa Brennan spoke eloquently of personal independence and isolation as the "foundational fantasy" of Western Civilization. I don't mean to collapse the distinction that Hannah Arendt drew between guilt and responsibility—but rather to remind us that responsibility permeates all aspects of a democracy. I may find myself a minority voice, or I may speak with an ignored voice, but we cannot disown those voices we abhor, nor can we stop speaking.

As much as I thought they did not, each of the four inaugural poems speaks to the fact that our history is awful and that our peoplehood is complex. It's interesting that two of our inaugural poets have been Black women—a constituency that has often found itself caught in the double jeopardy of a double oppression—but also an identity that often represents comfort and authenticity in the larger social imagination (think Oprah Winfrey).

So what did I want from an inaugural poem? The perfect marriage of politics and art? A lyrical ode to democracy? A radical attack on the brutality of our history? To be honest, I don't know. I actually gave writing an inaugural poem myself a shot, and it failed. Rachel Zucker and Arielle Greenberg invited one hundred poets to write poems for the first hundred days of Obama's presidency. I tried to capture the idea that a government and its people are in a difficult symmetry. The poem was clunky. So for the record: I could not do better. I took on politics as a poet, and I don't think I succeeded.

It's not clear to me how poetry and politics go together. It's easy to feel good about Robert Frost reading "Mending Wall" to Khrushchev or to feel bad about Ezra Pound's pro-fascist radio broadcasts, but did they really change anything? Were they substantive political acts, or merely decorative adjuncts to existing forces? Angelou served as the northern coordinator of the Southern Christian Leadership Conference following Bayard Rustin, but it's hard to think of "On the Pulse of Morning" as having a similar political impact. If politics is the art of the possible, poetry is the art of the actual. What one can viably say politically is often long anticipated by what one can say in a poem. My understanding of Audre Lorde's "Poetry Is Not a Luxury" is that poetry allows us to explore and discover what it is we will want to pursue and demand in politics. But even that keeps the two realms separate, not truly allowing for such a thing as a political poem.

In thinking that I disliked these poems, I allowed the bad habits of our political climate to inform my listening practice. I rushed to judgment; I substituted personality for substance; I read superficially; I listened to gossip rather than returning to the source. I allowed myself to make polar decisions of for/against. When I listened closely, I found a great deal to love in what I heard.

Now if only the rest of America would sit in their chairs long enough to listen. Even on a really cold day.

Postscript

This essay was written during Barack Obama's first term, and since then there have been two more inaugural poems: Richard Blanco's "One Today" (for Obama's second inauguration) and Amanda Gorman's "The Hill We Climb" (for Joe Biden's 2021 inauguration). I have also learned that there is a *semi-inaugural* poem, James Dickey's "The Strength of Fields," which was delivered at Jimmy Carter's inaugural gala, but not delivered at the inauguration itself. The texts of these poems are fairly accessible to anyone with Google, and I highly recommend them.

I have found this essay almost impossible to update, mostly because the place of poetry in the American imaginary has changed so much. My sense that poetry is a humiliated art in America has been turned on its head. At just twenty-three, Gorman was launched into actual celebrity by her inaugural poem. *The Guardian* printed the text of Gorman's poem under the headline "The Hill We Climb: The Amanda Gorman Poem that Stole the Inauguration Show." Gorman was not a closing act; she was a headliner. Gorman has appeared on the cover of *Vogue* and signed a three-year contract with Estee Lauder as their first "Global Change-maker" (Friedman, n.p). She has been photographed for *Time* holding a caged bird, a direct reference to Maya Angelou's memoir *I Know Why the Caged Bird Sings* (and the Paul Laurence Dunbar poem "Sympathy" from which Angelou's memoir took its title). I had assumed in the mid 2010s that poetry had retreated from the mainstream never to return, and that this retreat would be enacted by a disappointing moment of popular visibility in each election cycle that yielded a president from the Democratic party. Instead, poets have become stunningly popular, visible in a way that I don't think has been true since Allen Ginsberg was a household name. Sadly, I'm not built for fame, but if a showrunner ever wanted to strategically place my book on a character's shelf to telegraph the characters savvy taste, I would be thrilled. And I'll just put it out there that anyone thinks I ought to be photographed in Alexander McQueen for a magazine spread, and has the power to make that happen, I'm very easy to reach.

I have chosen to let the essay remain as it was originally published, even though I suspect that to younger readers, it will describe a poetry landscape that will most probably feels like a relic of the bad old days, when poetry (and capital-L Literature) was both balkanized and marginalized. Certainly, the distinction between slam, lyric, academic, and formalist poetry is not one that exists anymore, and if it does, the boundaries are more porous than ever. If there is any nostalgia to be had, let it be found in my sense of hope following Obama's election, when it really did seem like we had a chance to change the world.

Works Cited

Alexander, Elizabeth. *Praise Song for the Day*. Graywolf, 2009.

Angelou, Maya. *The Complete Collected Poems of Maya Angelou*. Random House, 1994.

Auden, W. H. *Secondary Worlds*. Faber and Faber, 1968.

Avant, John Alfred A. "Review of Just Give Me a Cool Drink of Water 'Fore I Diiie." In *Maya Angelou: Bloom's Major Poets*, edited by Harold Bloom. Chelsea House, 2001.

Bloom, Harold. 2001. "Introduction." In *Maya Angelou: Bloom's Major Poets*, edited by Harold Bloom. Chelsea House, 2001.

Brennan, Teresa. *The Transmission of Affect*. Cornell University Press, 2004.

Dickey, James. *The Strength of Fields*. Doubleday, 1979.

Friedman, Vanessa. "The Poetic Justice of Amanda Gorman's Estée Lauder Contract." *New York Times*, September, 2, 2021.

Gross, Terry. "Interview with Idris Elba." WHYY, *NPR.org*, 2011.

Hughes, Langston. "Let America Be America Again." poets.org.

Morrison, Toni. "Comment." *The New Yorker*, October 5, 1998.

Parini, Jay. *Robert Frost: A Life*. Henry Holt and Company, 1999.

Schneiderman, Jason. "Oracular." In *Starting Today: 100 Poems for Obama's First 100 Days*, edited by Rachel Zucker and Arielle Greenberg, p. 139. University of Iowa Press, 2010.

Stelter, Brian. "NBC Settles with Suicide's Family in 'Catch a Predator' Case." *International Herald Tribune*, June 27, 2008.

Williams, Miller. "Of History and Hope." poetryfoundation.org.

A Rising Tide Floats All Boats

Ten Lessons from a Quarter Century of Teaching

Even though teaching has become integral to my identity, I did not set out to be a teacher. When I set my sights on becoming a professor of creative writing, I thought of college professors as researchers and specialists, not teachers. I used to love cartoons and movies where someone assembles an elite task force to accomplish a mission—usually some kind of theft or rescue. I grew up fantasizing about being an expert, but I wanted my specialty to be poetry and poetics, not pyrotechnics or disguises. My attraction to creative writing workshops as an undergraduate was the way that we didn't start with a syllabus, the books and discussions predetermined according to some arc of history, but rather as we brought in poems, our professors held forth on whatever came up. I loved the moments when my professors seemed to go "off book"—suddenly giving a brief lecture on the line or voice or rhyme or identity. There was something spontaneous and unexpected to the creative writing workshop; moments of illumination and epiphany delivered with improvisatory skill. I still think of academia as a thrilling assemblage of experts. When I close my eyes, I see the faculty of American higher education forming an enormous *Oceans 11* style team of all human knowledge. I love that I get to be the prosody guy, just like I always wanted. I took seriously the root of "professor"—that one professed what one knew in front of a classroom. As I entered my first college classrooms as the instructor, I was excited by expertise and the sharing of knowledge. I knew very little about teaching because I didn't think of myself as a teacher.

Once I actually found myself in front of a classroom, I learned my first lesson about teaching: what makes you a good student often makes you a bad teacher. It's one thing as a student to be at the top of the class, but as a teacher, you have to teach to everyone in the room, not just the students who eagerly want to absorb your expertise so that they can follow in your professorial footsteps. My second lesson was that teaching is not doing: teaching poetry could actually keep me from writing the very poems that qualified me to teach creative writing. A third lesson was that the faculty teach what the institution needs taught. I wanted to teach poetry workshops, and I have. But I have also taught fiction, drama, and creative nonfiction. I have taught composition and literature. I have directed a writing center and trained writing tutors. I have worked with faculty on assignment design. I have worked with graduate students on job search materials. I have done what needed doing as often as I have done what I set out to do.

I was very lucky that early in my career, I was offered amazing mentorship in the realm of pedagogy. A graduate fellowship required me to spend time steeped in what is known as Writing Across the Curriculum pedagogy. Which meant two things. One is that I got to spend a lot of time with faculty from outside of the English department and get a far more comprehensive view of the student experience at the college. The second is that my required reading consisted of the greatest hits from the field of Composition and Rhetoric—or the field of how to teach writing to students. I highly recommend Nancy Sommer's work, especially on how students respond to faculty comments. John Bean's *Engaging Ideas*, the bible of the Writing Across the Curriculum movement, has been an amazing guide whenever I have been perplexed. I believe that the principles I lay out in this essay constitute an original contribution, even though they have been shaped by many other thinkers, and I have given credit as often as I can. I have relied largely on my own experience for evidence, which is typical of creative writers. I do fear that I will I not give credit where credit is due—that something recounted to me as common knowledge will have lost its origin, though I have tried to make sure that I have shown where the ideas have come from. My goal in this essay to impart what I know as succinctly as I can.

Each teacher is unique. You come to physical classes embodied, to hybrid classes on screens, and to completely online classes as text or videos. How students respond to you will shape you as a teacher. I learned early on that if I get upset, my physical embodiment of anger and frustration are funny to students. My best source of authority is to project a calm consistency. If I need to assert control, I have to slow my voice without raising it. I do think that there's a bit of a family romance to most classrooms. In my first classrooms, when I was is in my early twenties, I felt like my students saw me as a bit of a know-it-all older brother, left in charge while mom and dad went out, but not a true authority. Now that I'm older, I'm something closer to a fun uncle, and I suspect I'll soon be dad—and then grandpa. One year I was comparing notes on our student evaluations with a female colleague. In the written comments, a student had praised me for being so brilliant that I could teach at Harvard, while another student had scolded her for making her classes so hard she seemed to think she was teaching at Harvard. The same idea had surfaced as praise for me and insult for her. No one has ever commented on my wardrobe (and I make some interesting sartorial choices), while my female colleagues' fashion choices are often policed in the student comments. In my years of observing classes, I have seen firsthand that classes tend to grant more authority to men than to women, and to give less deference to faculty of color. Trust your instincts regarding your own embodied and disembodied authority in classrooms. If you want to be a teacher, try to teach in multiple settings and see where you feel most at home, and see where you feel most welcomed. Allow yourself to grow and change as a teacher as you grow and change as a person. If in reading this list, you think *that works for you but it will not work for me*, you may be right.

I often quote Mae West's classic jest: "I'll try anything twice." The earliest version of this essay was an attempt to make sense of my failures in the classroom, and many of the anecdotes remain in this essay, though now they feel less like failures to me, and more like the moments I learned something I needed to know. When I have worked with faculty on assignment design, I have asked them to see me as a thinking partner, and I offer these principles in that spirit, as an experienced teacher thinking alongside you. As a teacher, I see myself as a catalyst to my students' thinking, speeding their time to epiphany and realization. If I can save you time in becoming the teacher you want to be, I'll have done my job.

This essay lays out ten principles that I have learned from nearly a quarter of century of teaching. I have largely stayed within the confines of the English Department, though I've also had the chance to work across departments and disciplines. The anecdotes and stories are pulled from my own teaching practice, so they come from a range of courses, including creative writing, literature, and composition. There's also a touch of my work with graduate students and faculty. My hope is that in distilling what I've learned in the classroom, I am offering principles that will be useful in any classroom.

Know Your Learners

When I taught children's literature at my college, the students were mostly elementary education majors, and one of their favorite mantras was "know your learners."[1] I thought that this was excellent advice, especially as my students did not have the same goals for the class that I had. I wanted to teach them how childhood has been constructed throughout history, and how the literature that takes children as its audience can be studied as a sedimented archive of how children have been understood in different times and places. They wanted to know what books they should select for their elementary school classrooms. Knowing my learners, I included a two-week section in the middle of the course in which every student presented their favorite children's book. I had initially done this in the spirit of appeasement, but it quickly became my favorite part of the semester. The stories the students attached to their favorite children's books revealed aspects of their lives that created intense bonds within the classroom. This exercise also served my purposes by giving me a firm understanding of how they currently understood childhood and children's literature. I found it much easier to explain Mary Wollstonecraft's theories of child raising when I had a firm grasp of how it differed from their own baseline.

A difficulty with this particular principle is that you cannot know your learners until you have met them, and you will typically have to plan your syllabus and texts prior to the first day of class. You won't know where the students are unless you talk to them and read their work. I often leave some flexibility to my lesson plans, and I ask my students on the first day of class what they want to get out of the course and make a list on the board. Have your own list. See if they match. Do you have the same goals as the students? Can you adjust to them, or do they need to adjust to you, or both? Talk to your students about what they want and what you want. I teach a high number of international students who often have language acquisition as a goal for their classroom experience. How can I include language acquisition alongside literary analysis? Can I explain how what I'm doing in the class will match their interests? Many students come to class with no sense of the course's requirements, but an intense desire for a good grade, which is great! A good grading rubric will align the grade-oriented student with my goals almost perfectly. Explicitly asking your students what they want from a course can create a sense of trust and engagement.

Many years ago, in a literature class, I was teaching Raymond Carver's short story "Cathedral." In this story, the sighted narrator is apprehensive about meeting his wife's blind friend, but ultimately the narrator ends up having an intense and intimate relationship with the blind man. At the beginning of the class, the students were very excited to tell me that the blind man wasn't blind; rather, the narrator was blind. I asked my students, "Would you agree that it's wrong for the narrator to think that the blind man is deficient or less human for being blind?" The students agreed. I asked, "So we shouldn't use the word 'blindness' to refer to something that is wrong or deficient?" and the students again agreed. And I then said, "So why are we naming the narrator's inability to recognize the blind man's full humanity as blindness?" All of a sudden, I was watching the lights go on. (Another teaching lesson: just because the light *goes* on doesn't the mean the light will *stay* on.) My students got really engaged. I offered up the phrase "beautiful on the inside" for analysis and my students seemed to discover under my tutelage that sometimes, when we seek to overturn a value system, we end up reinforcing the very value system we set out to dismantle. My goal for the class was to challenge a kind of persistent ableism while also showing how our rhetoric can often reinforce the very values we claim to be rejecting.

But after class, as I was packing up, two of my students approached me and asked, "But in America you use 'blindness' when someone doesn't know something or can't do something, right?" As non-native speakers of English, they were very focused on understanding how Americans use English, and they were less interested in dismantling ableism than becoming fluent speakers of colloquial American English. I said that, yes, we often use "blindness" as a casual shorthand for various kinds of deficiency, but that I hoped they could see that this might be a problem because actual blind people are not deficient. A number of other

ESL students had gathered and I realized that I needed to also take their goals into account. Until I had met their goals of language acquisition, I couldn't meet my goals of challenging how that language is used.

I take an extremely structural approach to teaching creative writing. The line is a central obsession for me, as are the various structuring devices: end-words, rhymes, rhythms, forms. When I first started teaching creative writing, my teaching evaluations seemed split between those who were excited by my having shown them *how a poem works*, and those who were frustrated that I had not taught them *how to like a poem*. The second group baffled me. Why would anyone take a creative writing workshop unless they already liked poems? But over time, I have come to realize that students who want to be taught how to appreciate a poem can (and should!) be included in my more structural approach. Knowing my learners lets me reframe my goals to include theirs. I can build a workshop that includes both seeing how the poem works while also addressing how one might get pleasure out of the poem.

Create Shared Knowledge

You can never be sure of what your students will bring into the class, but you can be sure of the knowledge you build together in the class. I often start poetry classes with a poetry exercise that I call "Inside/Outside." I give students a packet of highly diverse poems, and they have to choose one they feel close to and one they feel far from. They have to list three things about the poem that make them feel close and three things that make them feel far; only one can be content. Tristan Tzara's "Howl"— which is the word "Howl" printed two hundred times before the line "Who still considers himself very likable / Tristan Tzara"—usually comes in for animosity. They hate this poem. It makes them angry. It makes them feel like the butt of a joke they don't get, and they almost all agree that he is a terrible poet. Usually one student will stand up for Dada, but not very well. I don't intervene. I let them vent their spleen on this poem, and even try to draw it out. Then, usually, a couple weeks later, a student in the class will bring in a poem using the same structure, with a single word repeated over and over, and the other students will think it's hysterical. They love what their fellow student has done with Tzara's work. They get the joke this time. After they are finished enjoying the parody, I point out how they have formed a reading community and that someone who had just joined the class today would have no idea why they liked this poem any more than they understood Tzara's poem on the first day. I then point out that the Tzara might need a similar context to be enjoyed. They organically realize that they have built a community and a shared knowledge—and that the literary world is a macrocosm of the microcosm we have developed. The shared knowledge means that they all move forward together.

As a student, I was very curious, and whenever anyone referenced something unfamiliar, I would run to the library to look it up. Sometimes it was very productive—it's how I developed my basic understanding of modernism and postmodernism. Sometimes it left me feeling a bit silly. A friend referenced *The White Shadow*—a late 1970s television show about a white basketball coach in a predominantly Black high school—and I ended up researching a literary figure that's often applied to mysterious doppelgangers in Edgar Allen Poe's work. When I first started teaching, I assumed that mysterious allusions or oblique references would stoke my students' curiosity as it had stoked mine; it did not. Rather, it made them feel insulted and insecure. I learned the hard way that if you want students to understand a reference in a literary text, give them the material beforehand so that they can go into it together with shared knowledge. Curiosity is a key quality for any budding scholar, but in most undergraduate classrooms, budding scholars will be the minority. Laying the groundwork first will bring the whole class through texts and exercises with much greater ease than trying to fill in the gaps later.

Development, Not Deficiency

If you are ever frustrated with a class, there is a corner of the teacher's lounge where you can find comfort. All sentences will start with "Can you believe my students can't even _____?" or "How can my students not even know _____?" You can go to this corner of the teacher's lounge (physically or online) for comfort, but I advise not staying there much longer than five minutes. Maybe ten if it's been a particularly bad day.

Here is template that has saved my life: "The next step is for you to _____." If I can introduce my feedback with that one simple phrase, I have moved from a model of deficiency to a paradigm of development. (If at all possible, avoid beginning feedback with "The problem is _____.")

My students often approach poems and stories as though they were life coaches who had been given a moral exercise: they are supposed to identify the good guys and the bad guys and say how the good guys should be rewarded and how the bad guys should be punished. Then they will say what the characters should have done differently in order to be successful. I was once discussing the Franz Kafka's *The Trial* with a student who was so intent on helping K, that he simply couldn't see that the power of the story is that there is nothing K can do. It is tempting to think of that student as *unable* to read Kafka, which would have allowed me to give up. But if I think of that student as *not yet knowing* how to read Kafka, then there is no incentive to abandon the student, and I can help him move forward. Interestingly, when I asked that student about his experience of the criminal justice system in the United States, it turned out that he had been to jail and that his court experiences were not so far from K's.

I sometimes explain to my students that they are in a developmental stage that it is time for them to outgrow, or if not *outgrow*, then build on. Certainly, students can still read a book by finding the good and bad characters, but they didn't need to come to college to do that—and at this point, they need to analyze the texts, not adjudicate them. And when I do work with adolescents or children, I respect their developmental stage. I do not try to make young people into tiny graduate students.

Sometimes in a literature class, I will ask my students why they are required to spend a semester watching fake people suffer. They usually think I'm having a nervous breakdown. They assure me that literature is very important, and when I ask them to tell my why, they offer tremendously inadequate answers. One class told me that we had read Suzan-Lori Parks' *Topdog/Underdog* because it taught them not to kill their brothers. I responded that if they didn't know not to shoot their brothers before that semester, I was extremely worried. But by having identified their current practice as a developmental stage that will no longer work, I can set the stage for them to grow.

Between Insult and Incoherence Lies the Sweet Spot of Learning

In theory, every activity and assignment in any classroom is designed to meet the student where the student is and then develop the students' skills while building on the students' knowledge. However, it's impossible to know precisely where every student is at any given moment, and in any classroom there will always be a range of skill levels and knowledge sets.

I find that if I pitch a lesson too high, the students find me incoherent. They simply don't answer questions because they don't understand what I'm saying. If I pitch the lesson too low, the students are insulted. The key here is not to avoid ever insulting or confusing a student,[2] but rather to know what to do in the case of each response. I have gotten very good at teaching my students scansion. I start with individual words and finding the stress, before building slowly to feet and meter. Now I can usually have my students scanning poems by the end of an hour class period. But if I began a class by telling every student to "write a line of iambic pentameter with a trochaic substitution," I would be met with blank faces. If I asked them to clap out syllables like a third grader, they would look at me like I'd just had a lobotomy. With any lesson, if the students bristle at the simplicity or are baffled by the complexity, use their response to recalibrate. If your students respond badly to a lesson, ask yourself what *your* next step is to recalibrate your teaching.

A key to this principle is the ability not to oversimplify or "dumb down" the material, but rather to break down the lesson into component parts. Make sure that you are laying a foundation that can built upon. It is useful to consider an often studied concern in the field of mathematics: student misunderstanding of the equals sign. In 1981, Carolyn Kiernan identified a problem by which students see the equal sign as meaning where to put the answer to a math question, rather than as a sign indicating a relationship of equality. Students learn that a problem like "4 + 3=_____" should be read as "write in the blank what 4 plus 3 adds up to." This can work for students for years if the teacher is only looking at the answers on math tests. But when the students see their first algebra equation, something like "4x+3=7" is incoherent. Then the students have to *unlearn* what an equals sign has meant to them and relearn what it really means to the discipline. I often think of this example when I am breaking down concepts to make them accessible for students. Be careful not to simplify to the point of misleading. Have in mind how each lesson will build to the next.

See the Work before the Class Does

There are two basic roles that students play in a creative writing workshop. As readers, they are developing their editorial acumen, and learning how to track their own experience as readers in ways that can then be made clear to the writers. As writers, they are learning how their work is received, what impacts they have, and learning to create the experience they want to create for their readers. Anything that interferes with those two roles does not belong in a workshop.

Sometimes the interference is structural. I once disallowed a student from workshopping a story in which he had given the main character his own name, and the characters in the story were the names of the students in the class. This character had given psychedelics to the class, and the story detailed the hallucinatory responses of the characters. I confirmed with him that he was planning to use the workshop as a kind of art project in which he was interested in forcing the students to talk about themselves as characters, rather than using the class as an exercise in learning to write a better story. That's an interesting project, but not the work of a creative writing class. Sometimes the interference is content based. I tell students that if I suspect that the class will be unable to respond to the work as a work that I will have a conversation with them about the discussion before we proceed. Recently, I disallowed a student from workshopping a play with extreme sexualized violence on the grounds that the authorial voice participated in misogyny. He understood when I explained that a male character in his play could call a female character a gendered slur, but the stage directions and character descriptions could not. Usually when I have discussions about content with a student author, they still want to proceed, and depending on the story, I'll sometimes preface our classroom conversation with a reminder of our roles so that we can continue to focus on the literary work as a literary work.

I have recently adopted Liz Lerman's Critical Response Process for my undergraduate workshops, which has been enormously productive. Critical Response Process is highly accessible, easy to learn, and keeps the author in control of the workshop. The four steps (Statements of Meaning, Artist as Questioner, Neutral Quesitons, Opinon Time) clarify the roles of the artist/maker, responders, and facilitator (Lerman). It also allows the author to retain a degree of control that that often gets lost in other workshop methods. Lerman's method is highly accessible and easily available (a quick visit to lizlerman.com will give you a clear overview and materials to get started). I have found that especially with difficult or shocking material, Critical Response Process keeps the roles of writer and responder on productive track, and prevents the pull of the sensational from deforming the workship.

Respect Your Student's Opacity[3]

I was once conducting a faculty training on course design focused on break down writing assignments for students into stages. One member of the faculty cohort was particularly distressed. From a diagnostic perspective, his problem was that his idea of rigor was the students being able to complete a ten-page project without guidance. For him to follow my advice and break the assignment into manageable steps would have made him think of himself as a bad professor, spoon-feeding his students the answer. But the students couldn't produce ten pages without fairly direct guidance, so he was stuck in a feedback loop of frustration that he had decided to take out on me. At a certain point, in exasperation, he shouted at me, "I'm the only thing between my students having careers in media and being drug dealers and prostitutes." I contained my laughter, but I was unsure how to respond productively rather than derisively. Finally, I said, "That sounds like a very heavy burden." I added, "I think that your students might actually make their own decisions as to whether or not they become drug dealers and prostitutes."

Beyond a number of gendered, racist, and classist assumptions on that instructor's part, I do think that many of us experience the weight of instruction more heavily that we should. I pointed out to him something I often pointed out to faculty: by the time students have reached college, they've had at least twenty teachers over the course of their education, meaning that each subsequent faculty member represents less than 5 percent of their experience with instructors. Certainly a great instructor can be life changing, and an abusive instructor can be shattering, but we should remember what a small piece we represent in the jigsaw puzzle of their educational journeys. We are often a much smaller part of their educational journey than we recognize.

I also think that his extreme comment was representative of a much more common faculty habit of projecting ideas and experiences onto our students that are unwarranted. I have often blamed myself when students stopped coming to class, trying to figure out what I said or did that made them stop coming, but when I have been able to follow up with them, it has never once been me that kept them from class. External forces in their lives that I wasn't privy too were the reason they stopped coming. I never want to stop being reflective about the impact of my teaching, but I also have to recognize that the private lives of students generally have more impact on how they conduct their studies than faculty input. Sometimes you can't ask questions that would violate the student/teacher relationship, but other times, you can probe areas that are baffling to you. I once had a group of students who seemed oddly resistant to writing fiction, and after a number of conversations, it turned out that as fundamentalists Christians, they felt that fiction was a form of dishonesty. It was not a problem I could have predicted, but once I knew what it was, I could help them meet the goals of the course. Part of knowing your learners is respecting how much about them you don't and can't know.

Let Students Be Experts

If at all possible, let the students bring what they know into class. This can range from asking them to explain a concept that they bring up in a classroom conversation to having students present on favorite poems. One of my mentors used to conduct teacher trainings, and she often pointed out that faculty have a tendency to make themselves a huge amount of work. Whenever a professor began developing some elaborate and time-consuming plan to address a problem, she would say, "Let the students do it. They're young and energetic. Take advantage of it." As I get older (and more tired), her wisdom comes into sharper and sharper focus.

In the same way that I often wait for four hands to go up before I have students answer a question (and I'll usually have all four of the students give their answer, just to bring all the voices into the room), I take advantage of the classroom space by asking questions that require students to put the answer on a chalk board or white board at the front of the class. We can discuss their answers together. It gives me a sense of where the class is as a whole, and gives each student a bit more context for their own progress. I also like to let students loose in poetry archives, finding a poem they like in an anthology or a podcast to present to the class (with clear guidelines on the presentation and a strict time limit). There's also a culturally determined response time to questions—ranging from up to minute, to negative time—in which you start answering before the question is finished being asked. For those of us uncomfortable with silence, and prone to excluding students who take longer to respond to a question because a quick response would be rude, having the answers up on the board lets all students bring their expertise to the room.

Teachers often say something along the lines of "there are not wrong answers," but I have found that every time I say that, a student will say something that is simply wrong. There's often an acceptable range of responses, but there are, in fact, wrong answers. Sometimes a student presentation or answer will be so outside the realm of accuracy as to need correction. More commonly, my disagreement with a student's presentation actually gives me the opportunity to open a productive discussion, and to treat them like an expert by illuminating the shade of difference between their understanding and mine.

Start with the Concrete and Move to the Abstract

This principal comes out of Writing Across the Curriculum pedagogy, and it's surprisingly counterintuitive. We tend to start with a principle and then move to the example, even though our brains prefer the opposite. I always start with examples of sonnets before I introduce the rhyme scheme, though I always have to remind myself to go in that order. (When I don't, I suddenly discover half way through Percy Bysshe Shelley's "Ozymandias" that his poem is a hybrid of the Shakespearian and Petrarchan sonnets, and now I've *really* confused my students).

There is no substitute for immersion. Imagine that you tell a friend that you are about to go duck watching. You explain that a duck is a sort of shimmering blue-green color, has two wings, two legs, a short neck, and a beak. You go to the pond, and your friend is doing a great job—he knows that a swan is not a duck, that a squirrel is not a duck, that children are not ducks. He consistently identifies ducks until a one-legged duck hops past.

"Look at that duck," you say, admiring the skillful hops that let it keep pace with the other ducks.

"That's not a duck," your friend says. "You told me that a duck has two legs, and that animal has one leg."

"Well, yes," you say, suddenly realizing that you are about to sound stupid, "I said that ducks have two legs, but that's a one-legged duck."

Literature classes are confusing for people who are watching ducks for the first time. The fact is that those of us who study ducks all day are more interested in the outliers—it's the one-legged ducks, the two-headed ducks, and the albino ducks that truly excite duck watchers. Somewhere between expert and novice, you have to recognize that all your descriptions of the duck were partial in ways that only another expert can understand. And I hope that this is not an ableist allegory—but rather a metaphor for what happens we don't take difference into account. And if we immerse students in the concrete before we give them the rules, they are more likely to include the outlying examples in their new conceptions.

Representation Is Not Endorsement

For the generation raised on the mantra "if you can see it, you can be it," the point of representation is to expand possibility. They want to see characters like themselves. I understand this completely. I grew up at a time when queer representation was extremely limited, and I was desperate for gay characters. I got very good at recognizing the coding of book covers for gay content and I often stayed up under the guise of doing homework so that I could watch VHS tapes of things like *Tales of the City* or *My Own Private Idaho* with the sound on low while everyone else was sleeping. We do need to see ourselves in stories to make sense of our lives.

But this ethos of expansive possibility can calcify into highly simplistic reading practices. For literature classes, this often means spending so much time condemning bad behavior, that nothing of interest can emerge. When I teach Almodóvar's *Bad Education*, I now start with a show of hands to confirm that we all find the abuse of children reprehensible so that we don't spend all of our time saying how wrong it was for the priest to abuse the character of the filmmaker as a child. When I ask my students if *Frankenstein* is a feminist novel, the unanimous answer is usually that it is not, because it lacks female agency and woman protagonists. In 1816, Mary Shelly, a teenager, having run away from her oppressive home to galivant across Europe with her married lover, wrote a novel in which two males (one clearly human, one made of human parts) behave so badly that they ruin the lives of the women around them. This does not seem to contain any female critique of masculinity for my students, who generally want to focus on how Victor is a terrible father, and what he should have done to parent the creature he brings to life. Feminism is hardly unitary, and it is my job to fully explore a feminist literary lens if I want to bring that concern into the classroom—but I am always surprised at how quickly my students need to critique the representation, as though the novel might not be written in such a way as to contain its own critique of the character's behavior.

For creative writing classes, this belief that representation is endorsement often surfaces in the desire not to make characters suffer, and to resolve conflicts in ways that are simplistic. The forced conclusions designed to show an audience what they *should* do in a bad situation remind me of the long-disappeared ABC Afterschool special (or more succinctly, the "That's one to grow one" vignettes of 1980s Saturday morning television).

Respect the Ego

Many years ago during a student conference, I was reading a poem that a student had handed me when I noticed a pinhole at the top of the page. The student had been having what we would now call a mental health crisis, and at that point my goal was to get her through to the end of the semester. The poem felt like code, and I had been about to say something about the way in which the poem kept me out as a reader, but the pinhole kept drawing my eye. Then I realized that this poem had been pinned up on a bulletin board or wall where the student would always see it. The paper's slight mottle and warp was from being on display. This wasn't a poem, this was a talisman. I realized that anything critical I said would be felt as a criticism of this shield, so I just asked questions instead, trying to draw out the meaning of the poem, careful not to challenge or diminish the work itself. I approached the conference by suggesting that the next step might be to write a new poem that would be accessible to a reader and communicate the poem's ideas to a stranger.

Poetry need not be more personal than any other form of writing, but it usually is. Giving feedback on poetry—especially to students new to workshops—can be especially fraught. While my student evaluations are generally glowing, the ones that are not often have to do with feedback I've given on poems. One student accused me of being unprofessional for saying that I didn't understand their poem. One student said that they should be able to say "that's just how I feel" when discussing poetry and that my efforts to unpack their opinions were unwelcome. Last semester, I was talking to a creative writing workshop about the difficulty of giving and receiving feedback on poetry. I complained, "Students will come to class, announce that they wrote a poem in four minutes on the subway on their phone, but if anyone offers any feedback that is the least bit critical they get furious and say *how dare you attack my soul*." My students smiled sheepishly, and a few of them said, "Yeah, we are like that."

One response to this is that I encourage students not to workshop anything that they aren't ready to hear discussed. Another response to this is to work primarily with exercises and assignments that take students out of a free flow of their feelings onto the page. I find that if there is something to discuss that is structural—how did this abecedarian solve the problem of the XYZ; how did this sestina solve the problem of repeating the same six words—then we meet one of my goals for the class, which is make the students see revision as inherent to the writing process. I try to take my own advice: I create shared knowledge to bring them to the next developmental stage of writing through exercises and assignments. Sometimes my students will object that I'm making them write in ways that they wouldn't normally write, to which I generally respond, "Yes . . . that's what school is. If you would do it anyway, it's not school." Which can sound mean at first, but really my larger point is I that am not *preventing* them from writing whatever they want to. They should be writing whatever they would normally write, and they will receive feedback on it—either in more advanced classes or in my office hours. I also explain that lower level workshops tend to assume that you do not have your own writing practice, but the more advanced the workshop, the greater the expectation that you have your own work that you will want to receive feedback on. An MFA workshop will consider whatever they are writing, but by then, they will have become far more skilled in giving and receiving feedback.

Because I teach so many foundational classes, I focus on exercises. I also tell my students that the great thing about exercises is that whatever they like they can keep, but whatever they don't like is my fault. It's their writing, so they can use it however they like in the future. And many more advanced students greatly appreciate the exercises as well.

As frustrating as it can be to teach students who treat feedback on their poems as referendums on their souls, I remind myself that it also indicates just how important their own poems are to them. That I have to find ways for them to be able to receive feedback and see poems as works in progress is only necessary because they are so attached to their own work, which means they do love poetry, and they do want an audience. Interestingly, this has also changed how I respond to more advanced students who are eager to receive critical responses to their work. To the student who asks me for brutal honesty, and not to pull my punches, I now respond that I will be honest, but that I'm not sure honesty has to brutal, and I certainly don't think poems should be punched.

Conclusion

A successful class is a rising tide that floats all boats. It meets the students where they are and develops their vision, while bringing them closer to achieving their vision. It allows students to enter with a variety of interests and skill levels and ultimately build a productive community. In the US, we often talk about education as though it were a series of instructions for putting together an IKEA dresser—that if we simply give (or follow) the right instructions, then everyone will reach a uniform end result, and we know in advance what that result will be. In truth, education is a form of attention, a form of engagement, and a form of growth. The nature of discovery is that you can't know in advance what you will find.

When I began my schooling in England, the students worked individually. For reading, we had a word tin with the words we needed to know before reading the next book, and once we could show the teacher that we had learned the words, we got the next book. Most reading was silent, but we took turns going to the teacher's desk and reading from our current book. I was very proud to be the most advanced reader, but I had no sense of deficiency in my fellow students. When I moved to California, my second grade classroom had four reading groups, and we all read the same book together out loud. The fastest and slowest groups met at the same time. I hated listening to students from the other group struggle through a paragraph or two of *Superfudge*. I kept my finger on where we were as a class, and zipped ahead. Instead of making us all better readers, the slower readers were publicly shamed and the faster readers were frustated. What I have tried to do in my own classrooms to create a social space of shared knowledge where we can all move forward together, though the more uneven the skill level of the students, the more challenging that becomes.

When I was still working out precisely what a workshop is for, I used to draw this diagram on the board:

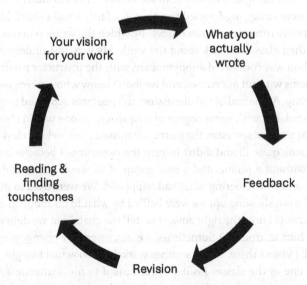

Fig05: A flow chart attempting to demonstrate the purpose of a writing workshop.

The idea is that you come to class with a vision for your work that has not been accomplished in your own writing. The feedback you receive helps you find a way to write the poem that achieves your vision. As you read the assigned poems and as you read each other's work, your vision—both what is *possible* in a poem and what you *want* to do in a poem—should expand. I would explain that I can't have a vision for you, but I can present you with poems that have been powerful for other readers, and as a class we can give you feedback that will tell you whether or not the reader's experience matches your vision for the poem. I no longer draw this diagram because in many ways I was working out my own theory of the workshop, and this was my way of making my understandings explicit. I might go back to using it. Now that I've dug it back up, I kind of like it.

I had not realized how chaotic my own undergraduate classes were until I began to reflect on how carefully I manage my own classrooms. I do wonder if I lost something as I scrubbed out some of the anarchy of those workshops. I was drawn to that chaos like a moth to a flame. Fights erupting in workshop were continued in discussions for weeks, but without being able to spill onto social media (which didn't exist yet), so we were struggling forward together in a fairly small cohort. My first classes were run on the "Iowa model" by which the writer remains silent while their classmates talk about the work. My very first undergraduate workshop was conducted anonymously, with the instructor passing out our poems without our names, and we didn't know whose poem we were discussing. At the end of the discussion, the poet was supposed to get the final word, but with some degree of frequency, no one would claim the poem at all. That semester, the instructor missed two weeks of class when he became quite ill and didn't inform the department because he lived alone without a phone, and a core group of us would come and sit in the classroom wondering what had happened. We were used to most of the class not showing up; we were baffled by what to do about an absent instructor. (I know the right answer is "tell the chair," but we didn't want to get him in trouble.) Sometimes we discussed our poems while we waited. I wasn't there, but in another workshop, an actual fistfight broke out in one of the classes (as it was recounted to me, someone actually leapt across the table to throttle someone). I can tell you for a fact that one of my college professors threw chalk at me for having a side conversation during workshop and shouted, "You're lucky! I used to throw books!" (I kind of deserved it, though I'm not sure it was a pedagogically sound exercise, and I have never thrown anything at a student.)

When I decided to become a creative writing instructor, I very much wanted to emulate the successes of my role models, and to "fix" what I saw as the mistakes of the classrooms I had not liked. But I also found that there was very little guidance as I entered the classroom, and what teacher training there was often went off the rails very quickly. (I kid you not that I was once in a breakout session where the leader kept saying "You have to *love* the students." My request for a clarification of what she meant by *love* went unanswered.) My biggest surprise about teaching is that it can be quite lonely. Students are not your peers; they are your students. Teaching a skill is not the same as doing that skill. Teaching can not only be isolating, it can keep you from doing the very work that you are trying to show your students how to do. You need support beyond the classroom and beyond your institution to keep you grounded and to offer you perspective. An earlier version of this essay detailed my early failures in the classroom, of which there have been many, and essentially tracked my struggle to find a pedagogy that would work for me and my students. This version tries to distill the lessons I've learned. I hope that this essay will be most useful for teachers who are just starting out in the classroom, or who feel like their pedagogy could use a bit of sprucing up, or who would like a thinking partner in reconsidering their workshop design. Many of my thoughts throughout this book return to my identity as a teacher; I'm not sure I would know who I was if I couldn't teach.

Education does not sit still. Today's discovery is tomorrow's common knowledge. Yesterday's common knowledge is today's debunked error. Yesterday's outlier becomes so representative as to be taken for granted. And today's assumptions will shift in endlessly surprising ways. Learning management software and online instruction have dramatically restructured our understandings of education in way that are only starting to make themselves clear. (I no longer tell students having side discussions that we can hear them; I tell them that they are not on mute.) We have to constantly recalibrate our teaching, depending on who our students are and where the field is. It's not easy to keep up, to remain reflective and curious, to keep our own values in mind as we adjust to a rapidly changing world, but we owe it to our students, and we owe it to ourselves.

Notes

1. I have been unsuccessful in finding an origin point for the phrase "know your learners." It sounds like an axiomatic truism, but the succinct and direct phrasing feels like something innovative and original. My students did not attribute the phrase, and I have found the phrase repeated without attribution in a good deal of educational literature, and I am following suit, though I certainly hope that if there is a single originator of the phrase, that a reader will direct me to this person's scholarship.

2. I realize that this could be read as my saying that students should be confused and insulted, which is not my intention. A student should never be insulted or confused on purpose, and my comments here are not about personal conversations but rather affective responses to course material.

3. My use of the term "opacity" here is informed by Édouard Glissant's *Poetics of Relation*.

Works Cited

Bean, John C., and Maryellen Weimer. *Engaging Ideas*, 2nd Edition. John Wiley & Sons, 2011.

Glissant, Édouard. *Poetics of Relation*. Translated by Betsy Wing. University of Michigan Press, 1997.

Kieran, Carolyn. "Concepts Associated with the Equality Symbol." *Educational Studies in Mathematics* 12, no. 3 (1981): 317–26. *JSTOR*. http://www.jstor.org/stable/3482333

Lerman, Liz and John Borstel. *Critique is Creative: The Critical Response Process in Theory and Action*. Wesleyan University Press, 2022.

Sommers, Nancy. *Responding to Student Writers*. Bedford/St. Martin's, 2012.

Notes on Not Writing

Revisiting *The Changing Light at Sandover*

Preamble

The Changing Light at Sandover wasn't planned out as a long work, but rather accumulated itself into being. The final work is composed of two and a half books, followed by a coda. The first installment, *The Book of Ephraim*, is a sequence of twenty-six poems (an alphabetical sequence, ranging from A to Z), and it appeared as a section of Merrill's 1976 book *Divine Comedies*. In this section, James Merrill and his lover David Jackson begin to converse with a spirit named Ephraim through their Ouija board. The following collection, 1978's *Mirabell: Books of Number*, found Jackson and Merrill being passed up the spiritual hierarchy from Ephraim to 741, one of a number of bat-like fallen angels, who begins to reveal to Jackson and Merrill the secret history and rules of the universe. Through the affection of Jackson and Merrill, 741 undergoes a metamorphosis from bat to peacock, even as he goes from number to person: 741 is happily renamed Mirabell by his earthly friends at the board, befitting his transformations. *Mirabell* ends with a revelation from the Archangel Michael that more lessons from higher authority will soon follow. Two years later, in 1980, Merrill published *Scripts for the Pageant*, in which the theology of the first two books is augmented, collapsed, and revised. And then in 1982, Merrill added a final piece to the existing trilogy titled *Coda: The Higher Keys*, renamed the entire work *The Changing Light at Sandover*, and printed it as a single volume. Three of the four iterations of the poem won major awards: *Divine Comedies* received the Pulitzer Prize in 1977; *Mirabell: Books of Number* received the National Book Award in 1979; in 1983 the National Books Critics Circle Award for poetry went to *The Changing Light at Sandover*.

Although the work appeared over the course of fewer than ten years, the time periods of the poems are vastly different. The events of *Ephraim* begin in 1955, when Jackson and Merrill were in their early thirties. By the end of the trilogy, they are in their mid-fifties. (And their facility with the Ouija board went beyond the confines of this large poem: in 1992, they conducted interviews with Henry James and Alice B. Toklas for *The Paris Review*.) In the first book of *Sandover*, most of Jackson's and Merrill's friends and relatives are alive. They visit, make demands, converse. As the trilogy progresses, the Jackson-Merrill social circle is increasingly on the other side, and those who had questioned the board now speak through it.

The final volume was a huge success, and at 560 pages, is an unusually large poem. The dust jacket of my copy boasts praise from Harold Bloom, *The Nation*, and *The New York Review of Books*. In *The San Francisco Review of Books*, Thom Gunn wrote of *Ephraim* and *Mirabell*, "I feel rather as if I were setting out to review *Ulysses* in 1922. . . . It is not that they are so difficult to understand as that they are so unprecedented, their ambitions so high" (153). On the publication of *Sandover* in its entirety, David Lehman in *Newsweek* said that "The result may well be the greatest long poem— and, at 560 pages, it is undoubtedly the longest great poem—an American has yet produced" (70).

I.

In one of the very last scenes of *The Changing Light at Sandover*, James Merrill and David Jackson are told by the spirits to prepare for a literary salon with the twenty-six greatest writers of all time. They are to set up the chairs in roughly the same arrangement as the letters on their Ouija board, and in each chair will be the most important writer to have a name beginning with that letter. From Austen to Yeats (the last seats are left vacant), the apartment is to be filled. The spirits dictate who will be coming, how to arrange the room, and how wonderful it will be. This ghostly audience is coming for a poetry reading to be given by Merrill. In the last line of the book, Merrill begins to speak for his spirit audience, and he ends with his opening: The word he begins his reading with is the first word of the *Sandover*.

By this late point in the epic, the spirit world's VIP treatment of the Jackson-Merrill household has become standard. What started out with tentative steps and hesitant revelations has devolved into the full reveal. Merrill is a prophet sent to save the world from nuclear holocaust; Merrill is made from the (second) finest stuff of the universe; if there's an important writer, Merrill's hand has been guided by him. In the first book, the spirit Ephraim is secretly in love with Merrill and Jackson, peeping from the beyond as they swim—but the affair is tentative and difficult. Ephraim initially demands their souls, but then retracts the demand as having been a joke. In *Mirabell* urgent messages come from the beyond. Mirabell tries to guide them through the intricacies of the heavenly hierarchy, but is constantly being censored, punished, and corrected. By *Scripts*, Merrill and Jackson have been chosen as the voice of God B (for biology) to communicate the truth of the universe. The demands and revelations give way to parties and back patting. Merrill isn't just universally loved—he's actually loved by the universe.

The Changing Light at Sandover jumps the shark roughly between books two and three. The dangers that stalked the lovers in the first books have been replaced by an endless red carpet rolled out from the spirit world, and the mythology—carefully built up in book two—begins to crumble under its own weight. The idea of reincarnation is introduced in book one, but by the end the recursiveness of rebirth has become absurd. Maria Mitsotáki (a dead friend) constantly complains that W. H. Auden has left her to go be with Plato, but then she reveals that she is Plato? And then after a visit by the nine muses, it turns out that they are all really just Maria Mitsotáki? The revelations become less revelatory. Ephraim is really Michael. The Mohammed they spoke with was actually a parody Mohammed. The "no accidents" clause is revoked. The characters lose their distinctive voices—and how could they not with the boundaries of identities melting away? The ouji board cameos from the recently dead increase in number and fame—including visits by Maria Callas and Elizabeth Schwarzkopf.

But that descent into ouroboros celebrity name-dropping is also marked by a certain abdication on Merrill's part. The spirits speak more and more and Merrill speaks less and less. We find Merrill leaving things up to the afterlife—as long as they can fill the page, why should he? This also seems to reflect the way of all things. The more notable change is that Jackson and Merrill are almost entirely absorbed within the spirit world. *Ephraim* and *Mirabell* pitch a tension between the living and the dead, between the material and the spirit. There are obligations, travels, surgeries, friends, parties, parents, and jobs that pull Jackson and Merrill away from the board. In *Scripts*, the connection to a social sphere is almost entirely severed. The ending seems to embody this development perfectly—it recasts the very book as spoken entirely to the dead.

What seems to hang over the *Scripts* is Merrill's age—Jackson's as well. There's a sense that everything that is going to get accomplished has been accomplished. Merrill set out to be a famous writer, and now he is one. Jackson set out to be a famous writer and his novels languish in drawers, unpublished. The potential for action and knowledge that drove the first book (and the lives of their thirties) have run out in the third because time is running out. Merrill and Jackson seem to have reached a point where there's just not enough time to change things. Without a mystery left to unravel, or a prophecy left to prophesy, the poem becomes a sequence of distracting parties, lacking urgency, lacking joy, buoyed by charm and little else (assuming you don't count the unicorn). The final section is built around twenty-five lessons, surely guidance for the living, but the lessons feel rote, unilluminating.

II.

I first read Merrill for a craft class that Agha Shahid Ali taught at NYU. Each week, having done the reading, I would come to class bewildered. Sometimes the explanations made sense. Okay, so I missed that the speaker of the poem was a window talking to a mirror. Or a mirror talking to a window. But sometimes the explanations left me more confused than before. Why write a poem where the first line rhymed with the last line, the second line rhymed with the penultimate and so on?[11] I still don't really understand the point of a rhyme if it doesn't even ghost itself into the reader's hearing, though now I have a great deal more respect for the poem.

My own breakthrough with Merrill came while I was listening to a Nina Simone album. I liked her voice, but I was impatient. I wanted her to hit the notes a little sooner, to speed up the tempo, to linger less. In reflecting on my frustration, I realized that I wanted her to be someone else—which would be impossible. If I wanted her voice, I would have to take the experience entire, to allow my chafing at her delays to be part of the experience. And once I trusted her to know what the experience should be, her voice began to open up for me in entirely new ways. I stopped chafing and thrilled to my bondage. A week later I pulled Merrill back off my shelf with the same determination to be patient and to trust. And Merrill's work began to amaze. At their own pace—a pace difficult to find in this internet age—Merrill's poems are dazzling fields of play.

Years after Shahid's class, I was looking for poems to teach in a workshop. One of my students had asked me to structure the workshop around the question of "how to write," and Merrill seemed like a good fit. He is a master craftsman, and his craft always inheres on the surfaces of his poems in visible ways. His prosody is never secret. It is never possible to reconstruct a writing process from the final product, but it is possible to see the choices that won out in the end. It is possible to see the accretion of craft, the carefully constructed cadences. Certainly, the question of how something was written is impossible to answer absolutely from the final product; but my hope was that by looking at the finished veneer, we'd be able to imagine our way into that process, and that imagined process, whether Merrill's or not, could become our own. "How did he get here?" seems a valid question for budding poets. Imagining a way to write can easily become a way to write.

Because workshops are so focused on the single poem as a form, I thought that it would be interesting to look at a long poem. I had wanted a large work—something along the lines of *Paradise Lost* or *Leaves of Grass*—something that we could read together as a group for ten weeks and neither tire of nor be overwhelmed by. I wanted to look at sustained writing over a long period of time. *The Changing Light at Sandover* easily lends itself to a division into five parts, so we could read *Sandover* on even weeks, different authors on odd ones.

And Merrill did not disappoint. Merrill's poems constantly call attention to their own composition. In one scene, Merrill and Jackson have been receiving a lesson directly from the Archangel Michael. Michael's teaching is that in addition to the five senses of people, God also possesses intuition, judgment, command, and pronouncement. At the end of the lesson, Michael announces his exit in the small caps that denote Merrill and Jackson's transcription of the Ouija Board: "SO NEXT WE DON

THE GLAD ARRAY / OF ALL OUR SENSES TO MEET THE DAY" (352). W. H. Auden now gets on the line, to complain about Michael's verse. He criticizes before trying out a revision of his own:

ENTRE NOUS MY DEAR HE'S NOT IMPROVING:
NEXT WE DON OUR SENSES IN GLAD ARRAY
& MEET HERE AGAIN ON ANOTHER DAY.
    (352)

Merrill responds, "That too could stand some work, if I may say so" (352). But Michael, archangel that he is, comes back and asks the two of them what they're talking about. Merrill stutters, flustered, but Michael seems more imperious than offended: "MY VERSE NOT METERED? NOT IN RHYME? THEN PRAY / MAKE SENSE OF IT YOURSELVES ANOTHER DAY." Then Auden and Mitsotáki swoon over the dreaminess of Michael, whom they agree is much cuter than his archangel brother, Gabriel.

Interestingly, Auden did have something to say about these sorts of voices from the other world. In his 1967 lecture "Words and the Word," the final installment of his T. S. Eliot Memorial Lectures, he distinguishes between the voices of the Greek gods and the "voice" of monotheism's God:

> As human beings, we speak in sentences made up of a number of words, and we must speak them in a particular language. So speak the gods in the *Iliad*, both to each other and to men. They make speeches, and they make them in Greek. But when the Elohist makes God say to Abraham: "Take Isaac, thine only begotten son whom thou lovest," we are not to think that Hebrew is the language spoken by God or that Jehovah, like Zeus, has vocal chords [*sic*] which make audible sounds. (116)

Auden continues this line of thought: "the Christian theologian is placed in the difficult position of having to use words, which by their nature are anthropomorphic, to refute anthropomorphic conceptions of God. Yet when such anthropomorphic conceptions of God are verbally asserted, he must speak: he cannot refute them by silence" (119). For Auden to be correcting and rewriting the language of Michael would put Auden on the side of the polytheist—making Michael, like Zeus, an embodied being with vocal cords—even if his voice comes through a cardboard frequency onto the Ouija board.

But then one ought not be surprised that Auden's theological ideas would be changed by dying. As Auden pointed out in life, to speak from beyond is to speak, and if the shade of Auden is to be every bit as anthropomorphically intact as Odysseus's mother in *The Odyssey*, then why not let God—or God B (for Biology) in Merrill's theology—be as embodied as the rest? Although, among embodied spirits, only Ephraim gets to enjoy the sensual pleasures of having nerve endings, and only once, early on in the volume. Merrill's Auden spirit even regrets poems and beliefs via the Ouija board, repenting that he "lookd for inspiration to / ritual and diffy moral strictures / so wrong" (164).

But to return from my somatic digression, what I want to focus on in this passage is how Merrill performs what looks like a writing process. Or how he performs on the page what looks like a record of revisions. We are given two versions of a statement, along with encouragement to continue working on the content until it can find the right form. Michael's statement is fairly banal—he's just saying goodbye and letting them know that he'll back tomorrow—but the discussion over how to say goodbye is remarkably fraught. Hierarchy, hurt feelings, revision, and desire all get mixed up in this clear display of the conflict between the possibilities of how something might get said and the actuality of something that has already been expressed. Auden's own formula from his lecture: "we do not know exactly what we are going to say until we have said it" (122). Writing and revision are not only processes of reshaping, but processes of discovery.

Much of *Sandover* is concerned with things that did not get written. The first book is largely about a novel that was never completed. Much of the last book is about writing the second book. Merrill continually offers the reader material that never made it to the page, except that if you are reading about lost material, then it is not lost. Merrill's books suggest—whether or not it was his process—that his writing is a kind of palimpsest, that the various histories of what he's writing are present in what you are reading. In fact, this is where we begin to feel the tension emerging between writing and not writing.

III.

Stephen Yenser in his excellent book, *The Consuming Myth*, addresses the way in which Merrill is always on both sides of every concern: "Merrill has been a writer uncannily alert to reversals and doublings. The duplicate and the didymous, the obverse and the inverse, the geminate and the specular are part and parcel of his art" (4). Yenser quotes Merrill: "Anything worth having's had both ways" as a starting point for understanding Merrill's serious flippancy. And this would seem to be the case. The more Merrill calls attention to his writing process, the more we become aware of what Merrill isn't writing.

In the first section, he's quite literally not writing the novel that he tells us he tried to write. But slowly, the messages from the other side increase, and we're aware that Merrill's writing is not writing at all, but transcription, dictation. David Jackson is given the epithet "hand" while Merrill is "scribe"—and Jackson is clearly the lower order. Whenever they are being evaluated, Merrill is just below Auden, Jackson just below Merrill. Auden is platinum, Merrill silver, Jackson an alloy of silver and tin. In this way, it becomes clear that Jackson's position as medium makes him less valuable than Merrill's position as composer. Or rather, it's not that one can do without the translator, but that the translator doesn't get to decide foreign policy. And yet Merrill is simultaneously insisting on his role as compositor while refusing that role. The more the reader believes in the voices of the spirits, the less the reader believes in Merrill's role as writer. If we accept the voices as direct communication, then Merrill is frequently downgraded to Jackson's role. One begins to wonder why the spirit world needs such a glorified secretary.

The search for material is a problem for all writers. As has frequently been pointed out, the best books that bear witness to history were written by people who were writers before they went to a war, survived the Holocaust, etc. Borges's famous formulation is that we have nothing but our dreams and our childhood to go on, though one wouldn't necessarily guess that from reading the work of Borges. I spoke to a colleague who had been on a search committee to hire a poet, and what had struck him was the length to which young poets write "project" books in order to secure enough material to cover 60 pages—whether the project has to do with a historical text, a biography, a scientific concern, or a personal event. Merrill's seeming solution is perfect in that it seems external and internal simultaneously. He simply gives us the voices that have intruded on his life. He simply needs to fill in the spaces between transcriptions. In an interview with Helen Vendler he admits his initial feeling was that using the voices in his poems "would be a kind of plagiarism, from whom I don't know, of what I don't know."

As the project moves forward, the voices of the spirits take up more and more room, and Merrill's Merrill-voice begins to feel more like connective tissue between posts from the spirit world, and less like a speaker who allows in other voices. Some of the best moments in the book come from the tension between the suave, camp charm of Merrill and the urgency of the voices when they first emerge. The very first lines of *Sandover* constitute a kind of anti-urgency:

> *Admittedly I err by undertaking*
> *This in its present form. The baldest prose*
> *Reportage was called for, that would reach*
> *The widest public in the shortest time.*
> *Time, it had transpired, was of the essence.*
> *Time, the very attar of the Rose,*
> *Was running out.*
>
> (3)

One would be hard pressed to find form and content that are in greater opposition. What more leisurely expression of urgency can there be than "Time, it had transpired, was of the essence"? But the voices that come from beyond are often filled with exactly the kind of pressure that Merrill can describe, but refuses to embody. When God B begins to speak through the board, the urgency is amazing:

> *IVE BROTHERS HEAR ME BROTHERS SIGNAL ME*
> *ALONE IN MY NIGHT BROTHERS DO YOU WELL*
> *I AND MINE HOLD IT BACK BROTHERS I AND*
> *MINE SURVIVE BROTHERS HEAR ME SIGNAL ME*
> *DO YOU WELL I AND MINE HOLD IT BACK I*
> *ALONE IN MY NIGHT BROTHER I AND MINE*
>
> (360)

Compared to Merrill's speech, we understand how urgent and clear God B's need to communicate is—and yet in order for the suspension of disbelief to continue, we can't believe that this is Merrill's creation. In the interview, Merrill maintains that he did progressively less shaping of the text as the work progressed; the voices simply came straight off the board in verse by the end. So if these transcripts are sheer reportage, how much has Merrill actually written? Is one answer to the question of how to write, to not write at all?

IV.

As the course went on, I ceased having much expectation of my students doing the reading—which was fine. One of the joys of private students is not having to grade them. If they don't do the reading, I have no obligation to mete out punishment. These were all adults with full-time jobs and families—it's not as though they were skipping the assigned reading to spend more time with some new gaming console. I encouraged them to dip in and out—to consider the poem less a marathon to be run than a pool to be waded in. I provided the narrative thread, kept them up to date on the comings and goings of the visitors and the build-up of theological rules. I did close readings of various passages. I checked out the assertions on physics. Here is an e-mail I sent to a friend with a PhD in physics:

In The Changing Light at Sandover, James Merrill receives this formula (through spirits, via a ouija board) for anti-radiation:
MO / RA : 279 / SOD
(SODIUM COMPOUND, MO MAGNESIUM OXIDE)
I just wanted to confirm that this makes no sense.

He responded:

To me it makes no sense. But without context one cannot be sure. He could have copied it out of some obscure handbook.

Which was enough for me to disregard it as a plan for when the bomb drops. I looked up the various religious references and names in Robert Polito's highly useful A Reader's Guide to James Merrill's "The Changing Light *at Sandover*". I found reviews from when the poem had been published in its various iterations, and found that the poem's critical reception was largely glowing, and that it is often discussed as an apocalyptic poem.

I tend to encourage my students to be irreverent—to find the flaw in the diamond and to regard the flaw as the most interesting part. In my own training, I found that my favorite teachers were the ones who didn't simplify the text, but rather the ones who made it more challenging. Because I often feel so dense myself, I find it comforting to be told that what one didn't understand is in fact strange. But also, finding the strangeness in what is said makes the text itself irreducible and necessary. If Freud or Whitman or Milton can simply be paraphrased, then why bother reading them—why not stop with the "very short introduction" series and call it a day? But if the original text is something that will continue to fascinate, something that can increase its strangeness with fractal-like expansions, then the original retains its value. And to recall Auden's earlier point, only monotheism's God is allowed to speak in pure information—the rest of us are stuck in the stickiness of human language. I would even be willing to say that struggling with language is what makes us human.

I tried to get my students to see how the voices from the beyond were being treated differently as the book went on. At first, they are tentative and timid. One has the constant sense of danger and risk in the first contacts with Ephraim. Merrill even contacts a doctor who assesses Merrill and Jackson as needing to figure out why they need a Ouija board to communicate their deepest feelings to each other. And the information from Ephraim is often upsetting:

NO SOULS CAME FROM HIROSHIMA U KNOW
EARTH WORE A STRANGE NEW ZONE OF ENERGY
CAUSED BY? SMASHED ATOMS OF THE DEAD MY DEARS
NEWS THAT BROUGHT INTO PLAY OUR DEEPEST FEARS
(55)

Though just as often, Ephraim brings comforting information about where friends and relatives are being reborn. Jackson and Merrill generally seem confirmed in most of their judgments. They are special; their friends are special. And of course the "no accidents" clause suggests a deserving quality to their respectively moneyed births, though Merrill was the richer of the two. James Merrill's father was Charles Merrill, cofounder of Merrill Lynch.

My own feeling is that the voices are approached in the first book, mastered in the second book, and kitschified in the third book. If my insistence on the kitschiness of the third book seems harsh, consider the appearance of Unice the Unicorn. But I don't mean to dismiss the third book as not worth reading, nor would I say that the kitsch isn't brilliant camp and fun. And it would be unfair to ignore the power of the ending, when the spirits call upon them to break the mirror and leave the spirit world behind. (I think the best parallel is how the second season of *Twin Peaks* became really silly before returning to brilliance at the end). Meryl Streep famously said that she won't allow her rehearsals to be reviewed because her process looks like bad acting. I often encourage my students to give themselves the same perspective—the writing process often looks like bad writing. But Merrill (Meryl? no accidents?) makes us believe that his process looks like good writing, in part by making it look like he hasn't written at all.

Socrates looked forward to questioning the dead when he arrived in the underworld. In the *Phaedo*, Plato has him say, "I believe that in the next world, no less than in this, I shall meet with good masters and friends" (15). In the *Apology*, Socrates hedges a bit, but still expresses excitement about the possibility of conducting his Socratic method with the great spirits who populate the afterworld. Roughly in parallel to Socrates, the divide between here and the after-here that gets blurred by *Sandover* is the same line that separates doing from not-doing. The question is just how much impact the spirit world can have on the material world. The otherworldly voices turn to kitsch as their ability to effect change on our world diminishes. When Auden starts to give instructions on where to find his final writings, he is punished for overstepping his boundaries. Similarly, David Jackson's father is censored before he can tell them where the bank books are. But the progress of *Sandover* is toward the spirit world viewing Merrill more and more as a tool for their own devices—as a prophet. But Merrill is a terrible prophet. He's no L. Ron Hubbard, drumming up converts. In fact, the friend (*a* Milton with no last name, not *the* John Milton) who truly believes in the voices from the Ouija board is a disaster: "Milton's ghastly on the spot / Conversion complete with rival spirit / And breakdown, not long afterwards" (87). The ghost of Maya Deren may be able to send dreams to prevent an American war with Cuba, but Merrill and Jackson can do little more than listen to the history of the universe. When Merrill asks Ephraim for the name of the baby his father's soul has been born into, Ephraim testily responds:

WILL

U NEVER LEARN LOOK LOOK LOOK LOOK YR FILL

BUT DO DO DO DO NOTHING

(38)

Once the line between the spirit world and the material world has become one of action, the question arises—what is writing? Isn't Ephraim's formula threatened by our knowledge that even looking is a form of interference? If speech is thought made visible, and writing is recorded speech (I'm tracing the Socratic ideas of *Sandover*), then in order to keep the line between speaking and acting in place, writing cannot be action. And if the spirits are not allowed to act in this world, then it seems that the spirits can speak (and DJ can channel and JM can transcribe) as long as it won't result in direct action. It keeps that line in place, while also enforcing "writing" as a form of "not doing." In Derridian terms, one might say that this distinction of thought and action is ripe for deconstruction—though Merrill is way ahead of me. Not only is Jacques Derrida David Jackson's acronymic inverse—JD and DJ, no accidents—but Merrill is already blurring the line. If the line weren't blurred, there wouldn't be so many censorings of the board. In setting up the difficult distinction, Merrill's entire poem becomes a meditation on precisely what it is that poetry can or cannot make happen. Auden is forbidden to try to manipulate the afterlife of his affects in a direct way, but Deren can indirectly prevent a war. Merrill sets up the question and answers it both ways. Writing isn't simply action or inaction, but rather both and neither. Or, more satisfyingly to me, writing, speech, and action are always proximate, at each other's edges, threatening to become one another. Persuasion and command are never as far apart as we might like to think. But whatever linguistic and logical knots this line of thinking may lead to, at the center of the paradox is Merrill, whose book represents a Herculean effort as well as a simple secretarial task. And again, we find Merrill as simultaneously one who writes and one who doesn't.

Auden's lecture from when he was alive proves remarkably prescient: "The artist is a maker, not a man of action" (118).

V.

In Alison Lurie's memoir of the Jackson–Merrill romance, the ends of Jackson and Merrill were far worse than I would ever have imagined. In the final years of their lives, Merrill and Jackson drifted apart—Jackson disgusted by the endless fascination with the Ouija board; Merrill's fame making increasing demands on his time. Merrill takes up with Peter Hooten and produces a video based on the work called *Voices from Sandover*, which showcases Hooten's acting talents. According to Lurie, the final piece cost over $800,000 of James Merrill's money (156). The video of *Voices from Sandover* has production values that lie somewhere between a college production of Shakespeare and an episode of *Dark Shadows*. The low point is when talking lips are superimposed over a picture of Wallace Stevens's face—a technology you may remember from episodes of *Clutch Cargo*. But while it's always easy to find fault with the technology of the past, the real problem is that the voices have more specificity on the page than they do on the stage. When Maria Mitsotáki complains that Auden has "FLOWN OFF TO PLATO POOR MAMAN, NOW WHO'LL / CARRY HER BOOKS AND WALK HER HOME FROM SCHOOL?" it's quite charming as a metaphorical description of her afterlife. But when an actress is actually pouting on stage in her best Greek accent, the charm is lost. Still, the interview that Helen Vendler conducts with Merrill following the production is fantastic. For me the most upsetting part of the production is that Merrill uses the Anglicized pronunciation of Ephraim as "EE-frem." I'm far more attached to the Hebrew pronunciation "ef-RYE-im."

According to Lurie, Hooten isolated Merrill from his earlier coterie, taking umbrage at old friends calling him "Jimmy" instead of "Mr. Merrill." It's an ugly portrait—Hooten comes off as a kept boy who fancies himself a Svengali. Back home in Florida, Jackson takes up with a series of toughs and hustlers who steal and scare away old friends. Faced with the choice between quitting smoking and lucidity (his brain is being starved of oxygen by cigarettes), Jackson smokes himself into senile dementia and fogginess. Merrill has AIDS; it seems unlikely that Jackson doesn't. As their lives slide further apart, they each descend into ugly prisons built partly out of vanity and partly out of time's cruel tolls on the human body and spirit. They die estranged, miserable, sick, fragile, and irascible.

VI.

My own supposition that the book is a meditation on mortality is seriously challenged by the fact that Merrill completed two more volumes of poetry after *The Changing Light at Sandover*. And biographically speaking, it is those works that ought to be saturated with mortality—but they are not. Retrospectively, it seems unlikely that Merrill could have known that he had HIV in 1982 when *Sandover* was published as a work entire. But in 1988, when *The Inner Room* was published, his HIV status was very much a death sentence. His final volume, *A Scattering of Salts*, published on March 14, 1995, came out five weeks after Merrill's death on February 6 of that same year.

But in that final book of poems lies the proper ending to *The Changing Light at Sandover*. Peter Hooten, interloper (to whom Merrill dedicated his 1988 volume of poetry), has disappeared, and Jackson is back on the scene. The Ouija board calls them back one last time in the poem "Nine Lives." As Jackson and Merrill worry about the cats that they're trying to adopt, Ephraim offers them the proof of the spirits' actuality and honesty. DJ and JM are to go to a cafe and wait. The spirits will bring them the newly reincarnated Maria Mitsotáki, now an eight-year-old Indian boy destined for a Nobel Prize. The two wait, but nothing happens. The boy doesn't show. In perhaps the most understated literary outburst since Flannery O'Connor's "Bailey turned his head sharply and said something that shocked even the children," David Jackson is parenthetically described as he "from whom burst certain long-pent-up reproaches" (600). Merrill points out to Ephraim that now they have lost "the proof. The proof we've never had / Or, mind you, sought. Proof that you act in our theatre" (600). Which is odd, since action has always been off limits.

Still, clarifying that Ephraim cannot actually *do* anything in this world restores the boundaries between the living and the dead. Any braggart who claims to be able to act from the other side will be humbled, as

Ephraim finally puts it, "mes chers we overestimated ourselves" (600). Once the other side can't act, our side—even as Merrill seems aware that he's not long for this side—is defined by action. Speaking, and by extension, the recorded speech that is writing, do not count as action. So in the end, the actions Merrill takes, with Jackson as his partner, are simply the quotidian motions of domestic love, set on the page in Merrill's careful, and in these terms, immortal measures.

Like Lurie—or perhaps because of Lurie—I want to see *The Changing Light at Sandover* as a love story. And in "Nine Lives" Merrill restores the centrality of JM and DJ to each other. The spirits which began as a bond between the two, but have turned into a third party, are finally expunged. Called upon to deliver they do not, and the domestic settles back over Jackson and Merrill, comfortably. The spirits have lost their ability to demand or command, and what is left is the daily work of living. My own belief is that love cuts out the bottom 30 percent or so of human suffering, and if we mark the end of *Sandover* in this final book, we find Jackson and Merrill back where we always hoped they would be. But then a few poems later, Peter returns. Merrill and Jackson's dog Cosmo has an "other Daddy" who turns out to be named Peter (650). A few poems later, "Family Week at Oracle Ranch" finds Merrill at a kind of wellness/therapy facility, described roughly as a benign version of the treatment center that Julianne Moore finds herself in at the end of the movie *Safe*. But is the speaker there with Jackson or Hooten? The name of his partner is never mentioned. So if there was no reconciliation in life, at least there was in poems—and the two take their places peacefully in the final collection.

But I'm not quite ready to give up in my reading of *Sandover* as a book that is shaped by an increasing sense of mortality. Though I do want to temper my argument. I think that the confrontation with death that I've argued for in book three is a successful one. Having confronted mortality, Merrill comes through it, and the final two collections reflect a knowledge of death that does not preclude creativity or work. In fact, they reflect a wisdom and a calm that seem impossible without the crisis brought about in *Sandover*. Lurie reports that in 1990 Merrill said to her, "I'm afraid Death is beginning to be interested in me" (169). Despite how clearly *Sandover* represents death's threshold as a two-way turnstile, it seems that outside the poems, JM confronted mortality in the traditional way, too.

Coda

At the end of the class, I had hoped for us to make a Ouija board and contact James Merrill and Ephraim, but it quickly became clear that that would be a bad idea. My own two experiences with Ouija boards have been mixed. Once a friend was so badly disturbed by contacting his grandfather that he kept me awake all night, and I had to catch a plane in the morning. He'd been operating the board with a friend who maintained that she had been born into a line of Wiccan priestesses, and while I hadn't been in the room during his conversation with the afterworld, I felt rather disgruntled at having to suffer the consequences. The other time, I was rather sincerely trying to contact a spirit who seemed to be haunting me, but the planchette remained stubbornly still. I'd been hoping for a third option—something between nothing and panic, but I'm no James Merrill, and I suspected that we'd be left with one or the other.

I'd started the class with a writing exercise in which my students paired off and took turns being a spirit voice. They'd write questions and then switch notebooks, writing in the small caps and shorthand abbreviations of Merrill's voice when being the spirit. But they found the exercise unproductive in the end. Either the other voice spoke in the wrong register, offering the wrong worldview for their own poems, or they wanted back the language they were giving away. I had hoped that they, like Merrill, would be able to experiment with not writing, but not surprisingly, since they'd come to class to learn to write, they didn't want to not write. Merrill's success with *Sandover* rests on a sequence of paradoxes and an embrace of opposites. But for me, more than anything, it's a powerful meditation on not writing—on receiving text, or making text seem received. Carolyn Forché, famously, in "The Colonel" says, "There is no other way to say this," but of course there's always another way.[2] The genius of Merrill is to put the other way out of reach, even while making it visible. He shows us what could have been written, while simultaneously refusing and accepting responsibility for the voices that (to varying degrees) compose the poem. When I first began to realize that I was thinking about *Sandover* as a meditation on not writing, I felt a bit disturbed. Considering the cult of Merrill, this thought seemed a bit blasphemous. But as I grew attached to the idea, it felt like praise, not criticism.

I've never really believed in writer's block, mostly because it suggests a metaphor of a pipeway or a stream. If one can't write, in the world of "writer's block," then there's simply an obstruction that needs to be removed. It suggests that the natural state for all people is to be writing, all the time, with nary a pause. It suggests an endlessly renewing reservoir of writing that already exists inside each writer, which I find an absurd form of fatalism. Certainly, a discipline of writing is quite useful. But I find that "dry spells" (how I think of them—it's not that there's too much in the reservoir, but too little) can be calm and pleasant or frustrating and terrifying. Sometimes, when the poetry isn't coming, I feel a bit like an actor between parts—trusting that something will come along, but also on the lookout for the next production. In thinking about Merrill's masterpiece as a masterwork of not writing, I find a certain satisfaction in how work can come from unlikely, unexpected, or feared places. In some ways, it's a conceptual work. We can't all run to our Ouija boards, but certainly it's not *that* far from the experiments by Flarf or the Conceptual Writers. As KG said in *Poetry*, "With so much available language, does anyone really need to write more?" (315). My hope is that yes—we'll always need to write more. But my other hope is that our writing will encompass more than we can initially conceive, including not writing.

It's also the case that we are often compelled to write what we would prefer not to. Toward the end of *Mirabell*, Merrill complains

Here I go again, a vehicle
In this cosmic carpool. Mirabell once said
He taps my word banks. I'd be happier
If I were tapping them. Or thought I were.
    (262)

Again, in *Scripts*, in an interchange with Robert Morse, he tries to turn off the faucet:

Stop, we must pack for Venice! And friends already
Plead for no more big speeches in small caps.
    (499)

Many writers describe those wonderful days when they are simply "in the zone"—when everything seems primed and ready, and great work just flows right out. In the classical Greek notion of "inspiration" one literally inhales the Gods, or the muses work directly through the artist. Perhaps "not writing" can also be that compulsion. Beginning writers are often asked if they could stop writing if they wanted to. (The correct answer, beginning writers, is "no.") In many ways, this compulsion to write, rather than the decision to write, is what I've meant by not writing. Which, paradoxically, would mean that our best writing is not.

Notes

1. The answer is that the form mimics the accretion of layers that builds a pearl; the poem is entitled "Pearl."

2. Mark Doty's definition of poetry, as he lays it out in *Still Life with Oysters and Lemon*, is instructively similar: "What makes a poem a poem, finally, is that it is unparaphrasable. There is no other way to say exactly this" (70). It's the very essence of poetry itself that Merrill is calling attention to.

Works Cited

Doty, Mark. *Still Life with Oysters and Lemon: On Objects and Intimacy.* Beacon Press, 2001.

Forché, Carolyn. "The Colonel" (1981). In *The Wadsworth Anthology of Poetry*, ed. Jay Parini. Thomson Wadsworth, 2006.

Gunn, Thom. "A Heroic Enterprise." *San Francisco Review of Books*, August 1979. Reprinted in Robert Polito, *A Reader's Guide to James Merrill's The Changing Light at Sandover*.

James Merrill: Voices from Sandover. Dir. Joan Darling. Perf. Peter Hooten, James Merrill. Films for the Humanities, 1990.

K. G. "Introduction to Flarf and Conceptual Writing." *Poetry* 194, no. 4 (2009): 315.

Lehman, David. "Merrill's Celestial Comedy: *The Changing Light at Sandover*." *Newsweek*, February 28, 1983. Online, LexisNexis Academic.

Lurie, Alison. *Familiar Spirits: A Memoir of James Merrill and David Jackson.* Viking, 2001.

Merrill, James. *The Changing Light at Sandover with the Stage Adaptation Voices from Sandover*, ed. J. D. McClatchy and Stephen Yenser. Knopf, 2006.

Merrill, James. *Collected Poems*, ed. J. D. McClatchy and Stephen Yenser. Knopf, 2001.

Merrill, James. Interview by Helen Vendler. *James Merrill: Voices from Sandover*. Films for the Humanities, 1990.

Plato. *Phaedo*, trans. F. J. Church/Macmillan, 1951.

Polito, Robert. *A Reader's Guide to James Merrill's "The Changing Light at Sandover."* University of Michigan Press, 1994.

Yenser, Stephen. *The Consuming Myth: The Work of James Merrill*. Harvard University Press, 1987.

The Loved One Always Leaves

The Poetic Friendship of Agha Shahid Ali and James Merrill

Saying that James Merrill and Agha Shahid Ali were friends is a bit like saying that Auguste Rodin and Rainer Maria Rilke were friends—it fails to do justice to the intensity of the relationship, and it fails to capture the enormous influence of the senior partner on the junior partner. Ali's first book, *The Half-Inch Himalayas*, appeared in the same year that the two met. The collection is marked by free verse and a light touch, with an epigraph from Virginia Woolf: "for wherever I seat / myself, I die in exile." Ali opened his literary career with Woolf's idea of symbolic death. Fifteen years later, facing his own literal death from brain cancer, Ali closed his penultimate book of poems by letting Merrill guide him into the afterlife. Virginia Woolf and T. S. Eliot were Ali's high modernist precursors—the touchstones he turned to as a scholar and young writer; Merrill was his real-life mentor, a flesh-and-blood friend, and a powerful influence whose example led Ali both toward the increasing formalism that opened out onto his embrace of the ghazal, as well as his guide into an untimely death.

Agha Shahid Ali and James Merrill met at a dinner party in Arizona, where Ali had asked to prepare a meal to meet the visiting poet. Shahid was almost instantly beloved by everyone who met him, and Merrill was no different. That single dinner party in Arizona led to an affectionate and loving correspondence, in which they quickly adopted the roles of literary *erastes* and *eramonos*. Amitav Ghosh recalled that after befriending Merrill, Ali "began to experiment with strict metrical patterns and verse forms such as the canzone and the sestina" (313–14). Critics have

associated Ali's Merrill-inspired turn toward form with his poetic matu-
ration (Newman, par. 1); by the end of the 1990s, Ali had become strongly
identified with formal poetry and the formal ghazal in particular.

Alison Lurie's account of Merrill's life suggests that Merrill's final years
were marked by dissolution: his relationship to Peter Hooten had eclipsed
his partnership with David Jackson, and Jackson was taking increasing
risks in is own sexual escapades. However, Merrill's poems and the smat-
tering of his letters that I have seen suggest that Merrill had found something more like a molecular structure of sex and affection that linked his
various relationships into a web of care, rather than a nexus of betrayal
and recrimination.

While it is clear that Merrill's influence on Ali was profound, there
are a number of red herrings. Shahid's 1987 chapbook *A Walk Through the
Yellow Pages* would seem to pay an obvious homage to Merrill's 1974 book
The Yellow Pages, but there is no relation in form or content that I can
discern beyond the title. Both collections are heavy with allusion, though
Agha writes about fairy tales while Merrill's references are mythological
and historical. Considering that the two only met in 1987, Ali's choice of
title seems an aspirational association with Merrill, if anything.

More interesting than picking about in Ali's work for the influence
of James Merrill is considering how their careers as poets both turned
on unlikely obsessions that came to dominate their poetry and their
reputations. One can hardly think of Merrill without the Ouija board
at which he and David Jackson entertained their "visitors." These com-
munications via Ouija formed the heart of *The Changing Light at Sandover*, which earned Merrill a Pulitzer, a National Book Award, and the
National Book Critics Circle Award (although the awards accumulated
as the poem was published in its component parts). This long poem
remains a landmark of American literature, though it is somewhat aloof
from Merrill's other work.

Ali's rehabilitation of the ghazal in English both restored the formal
constraints for the English language reader and insisted on a historical
dignity for the form that it had been denied in the West. In the introduction to his anthology of ghazals, *Ravishing Disunities*, Ali rejects Paul
Oppenheimer's claim that the sonnet is the oldest poetic form still in use,
pointing out that the ghazal originated in the eleventh century (*Ravish-*

ing, 1). While the formal constraints of the ghazal have been known to English-language readers and writers since at least the 1930s, and the ghazal seemed dormant in the 1940s and 1950s, the free-verse translations of the Indian poet Ghalib (most notably by Adrienne Rich) in the 1960s created the perception that ghazals were simply free-verse poems in which unrelated couplets were unified by no more than mood or tone. Ali restored the formal constraints of the ghazal, offering English-language writers a form that could avoid the unities of narrative or argument, and allow a multifaceted approach to a single subject, like exile or rain. A posthumous collection of Ali's ghazals, *Call Me Ishmael Tonight*, appeared in 2003. Twelve years later, it is almost impossible to discuss the ghazal in English without acknowledging Ali's codification and popularization of the form in English.

In finding these new modes—Merrill at his Ouija board and Ali at the ghazal—they intensified the power of their work. One way to see the trajectory of Merrill's *Sandover* is toward an aesthetics of transcription—a paradoxical refusal of the sort of formal shaping that poetry demands, as the voices are increasingly *received* through the Ouija board. Of course, the voices collapse on themselves, reincarnation allowing each speaker to reveal himself as an incarnation of another speaker. Merrill's work after *Sandover* feels more relaxed than what had come before. By Merrill's last collection, *A Scattering of Salts*, the poems are still formal, but they somehow feel less self-conscious. Just as Merrill's switch from glasses to contacts removed a barrier between himself and the world, so the later poems feel like conversations, rather than revelations.

In speaking of his attachment to Ali's work, Amitav Ghosh wrote: "His voice was like none I had heard before. . . . His was a voice that was not ashamed to speak in a bardic register. I could think of no one else who would even conceive of publishing a line like: 'Mad heart, be brave'" (31). This mode of bardic intensity was facilitated by the ghazal because those moments no longer had to be embedded in stories or linear meditations. The last ghazal of Ali's final book, *Call Me Ishmael Tonight*, is one couplet, declaiming in precisely the voice that attracted Ghosh: "If you leave who will prove that my cry existed? / Tell me what was I like before I existed" (84).

Though twenty-three years Merrill's junior, Ali only survived Merrill by six years. Still, in perhaps his most interesting act of devotion and influence, Ali inhabited Merrill's technique of ventriloquism when he himself faced the void. Just as Merrill had channeled his mentors and guides (particularly W. H. Auden) through the Ouija board, now Ali summoned Merrill in his poetry. Ali's penultimate collection, *Rooms Are Never Finished*, narrates his journey to Kashmir with his family in order to bury Shahid's beloved mother. In the final poem of the book, "I Dream I Am at the Ghat of the Only World," Ali blends multiple mythologies and cultures as he boards a dreamlike boat and attempts to make peace with his loss. Merrill's voice appears in all capital letters, the same technique used to indicate communication through the Ouija board in *Sandover*, as Merrill guides Shahid in coping with both his mother's and his own mortality.

It was no mistake that Ali chose Merrill to guide him into the next world. As a scholar of T. S. Eliot, Ali must have been familiar with this passage from "Tradition and the Individual Talent": "No poet, no artist of any art, has his complete meaning alone. His significance, his appreciation is the appreciation of his relation to the dead poets and artists. You cannot value him alone; you must set him, for contrast and comparison, among the dead" (101). Merrill had secured his place in the tradition by relating himself to his immediate predecessors in *Sandover*. At the end of his life, Ali makes the same move, both anchoring himself to the tradition, but also insisting on securing Merrill's place there. Merrill becomes his Virgil, and Ali makes himself his own Dante.

At the end of a book about a journey to bury his mother, one might expect Merrill to arrive with a prophecy regarding where Ali's mother would about to be reincarnated. Reincarnation is the primary obsession of *Sandover*. However, Merrill's voice arrives with no comfort based in the afterlife: "SHAHID, HUSH. THIS IS ME, JAMES. THE LOVED ONE ALWAYS LEAVES" (104). Merrill delivers comfort in the form of the universality of suffering. Shahid should quiet his tears not because his loss serves a celestial plan, or because his mother will soon be returned to the Earth, but because loss is the foundational condition of life. Indeed, Merrill is perhaps *less* lost in that his voice can come to comfort Ali, while his mother remains unreachable in the afterlife. But the truth Merrill offers to Ali is simply that we must all bear loss, no matter whom we love.

Coda

In writing this, I'm struck by how hyperbolic my own memory of Shahid has become. I was in his craft class at NYU in the fall of 2000, and I distinctly remember him telling us that the problem with young poets is that they have never spent ten years working on a poem and therefore do not trust that a poem will work itself out given time. As an example, he told us about the poem "Eurydice," the opening poem of *A Nostalgist's Map of America*. He had wanted to write a poem about Eurydice in a contemporary place, and one morning after a run, he realized that she was in a concentration camp—it allowed for the same overpowering forces to tear away the beloved after a hard won reunion. And yet, here is Christine Benvenuto in the *Massachusetts Review*, "One poem, the haunting epigraph to *Nostalgist's Map* called 'Eurydice,' took a year" (263). Why do I remember ten?

Similarly, I swear that I remember Shahid telling us that he wrote to Merrill, asking him if it was okay to rhyme, and that in response, Merrill sent him a rhyming dictionary. But Shahid's brother told me that I misremembered the story, and in an interview, Shahid describes the conversation I was referencing as having been part of a long discussion with Merrill about rhyme. Merrill had vetoed certain of Ali's rhymes: "seem" and "scene" were not acceptable, but "clean" and "scene" were a good pair. "And then he said, 'Do you have a rhyming dictionary? No? I'll send you one.' And I said, 'Send me the rhyming dictionary.' I revised the poem according to his strictures and called me to congratulate me about the rhymes I had" (Maring, 65). The recently published letters of James Merrill give us the exact moment. In a letter to Shahid dated October 30, 1992, Merrill writes "My dear—do you have a rhyming dictionary? . . . Let me know. I will be happy to send you. + and it can remain 'our little secret.' Now don't pout." This letter also contains Merrill's advice on rhyming: "I must scold you on your irresponsible rhymes. . . . Get off the fence + decide what your rhyme word [is] and stick to it." (The editorial insertion of "is" comes from editors Langdon Hammer and Stephen Yenser.)

I wish I could say that I come here to mythologize Shahid, rather than to analyze his work or his friendship with James Merrill—that I could write the sort of effusive and hyperbolic encomium that I carry with me every day. The lore that has built up around Shahid is fantastic and beautiful. I remember visiting him in the hospital, and then at his home in Brooklyn, and I remember the moment when I received the news of his death. Attending his memorial service reminded me both of how much we had lost and how much we could keep. Time is a great sieve, and the smaller things are lost as we move forward. Perhaps it is only by making the memories larger than life that we can be sure that they will last longer than we do.

Merrill wrote a world in which nothing is lost because everyone is always coming back, and Shahid wrote a world in which loss can be borne because it is universal. Literature, it seems to me, strikes a balance between those two. Certainly, much is lost, constantly—yet much remains. Ali Shahid Ali and James Merrill seem assured of future readers, and like John Keats or Emily Dickinson, will be loved for their biographies as well. In my own friendship with Shahid, I feel a small kinship with Merrill. The loved one may always leave, but thanks to poetry, he will always *also* persist.

Works Cited

Ali, Agha Shahid. *Bone-Sculpture: Poems.* Writers Workshop, 1972.
Ali, Agha Shahid. *Call Me Ishmael Tonight: A Book of Ghazals.* Norton, 2004.
Ali, Agha Shahid. *The Half-Inch Himalayas.* Wesleyan University Press, 1987.
Ali, Agha Shahid. *In Memory of Begum Akhtar.* Writers Workshop, 1979.
Ali, Agha Shahid. *A Nostalgists Map of America.* Norton, 1992.
Ali, Agha Shahid. *Rooms Are Never Finished.* Norton, 2002.
Ali, Agha Shahid. *A Walk Through the Yellow Pages.* SUN/Gemini Press, 1987.
Ali, Agha Shahid, Ed. *Ravishing Disunities.* Wesleyan University Press, 2000.
Benvenuto, Christine. "Agha Shahid Ali." *Massachusetts Review* 43, no. 2 (2002): 261–68. Humanities Full Text (H. W. Wilson).
Eliot, T. S. "Tradition and the Individual Talent." *The Waste Land and Other Writings.* The Modern Library, 2001.
Ghosh, Amitav. "'The Ghat of the Only World': Agha Shahid Ali in Brooklyn." *Postcolonial Studies* 5, no. 3 (2002): 311–23.
Gussow, Mel. "James Merrill Is Dead at 68; Elegant Poet of Love and Loss." *New York Times*, February 7, 1995, Late Edition, sec. B. Print. LexisNexis.
Low, Bernadette Flynn. "Agha Shahid Ali." *Guide to Literary Masters & Their Works* (2007): 1. Literary Reference Center.

Lurie, Alison. *Familiar Spirits: A Memoir of James Merrill and David Jackson.* Viking, 2001.

Maring, Heather. "Conversation with Agha Shahid Ali." *Center: A Journal of the Literary Arts* 1, no. 2 (2002): 57–69. Literary Reference Center.

Merrill, James. *Collected Poems.* Ed. J. D. McClatchy, and Stephen Yenser. Knopf, 2001.

Merrill, James. *The Changing Light at Sandover with the Stage Adaptation Voices from Sandover.* Edited by J. D. McClatchy and Stephen Yenser. Knopf, 2006.

Merrill, James. *A Whole World: Letters from James Merrill.* Edited by Langdon Hammer and Stephen Yenser. Knopf, 2021.

Newman, Amy. "Separation's Geography: Agha Shahid Ali's Scholarship of Evanescence." *Hollins Critic* 43, no. 2 (2006): 1–14. Literary Reference Center.

Pace, Eric. "Agha Shahid Ali, 52, a Poet Who Had Roots in Kashmir." *New York Times*, December 26, 2001, Late Edition, sec. C. Print. LexisNexis.

Reece, Spencer. "Remembering James Merrill." *Boulevard* 22, 2/3 (2007): 1–31. *Literary Reference Center*, August 25, 2013.

Schneiderman, Jason. "Notes on Not Writing: Revisiting *The Changing Light at Sandover*." *The American Poetry Review* 38, no. 5 (2009): 15–21.

Acknowledgments

Poems

Julia Alvarez, "Let's make a modern primer for our kids," and "Mami asks what I'm up to, and that means men," from "33," from *HOMECOMING*. Copyright © 1984, 1996 by Julia Alvarez. Published by Plume, an imprint of Penguin Random House; originally published by Grove Press. By permission of Stuart Bernstein Representation for Artists, New York, NY and protected by the Copyright Laws of the United States. All rights reserved. The printing, copying, redistribution, or retransmission of this Content without express permission is prohibited.

Ada Limón, "State Bird" from *Bright Dead Things*. Copyright © 2015 by Ada Limón.

Reprinted with the permission of The Permissions Company, LLC on behalf of Milkweed Editions, milkweed.org.

Jennifer Knox, "The Decorative Airport Fern Is Not What It Pretends to Be" © 2011 Jennifer L. Knox, reprinted from *Days of Shame & Failure* (Bloof Books) by permission of the author.

Cover Art

Michael St. John, "Box." Used by permission of the artist.

Acknowledgments